BEHOLD
MY HEART

BEHOLD MY HEART

THE LIFE AND LEGACY OF AUGUSTINE

JOSHUA J. CONGROVE

WARHORN MEDIA
BLOOMINGTON, INDIANA

WARHORN MEDIA
2401 S Endwright Rd.
Bloomington, Ind. 47403
WARHORNMEDIA.COM

© 2021 by Joshua J. Congrove. All rights reserved.

Printed in the United States of America

ISBN-13: 978-1-940017-38-9 (paperback)
ISBN-13: 978-1-940017-39-6 (PDF)
ISBN-13: 978-1-940017-40-2 (EPUB)
ISBN-13: 978-1-940017-41-9 (Kindle)

Design by Alex McNeilly. The cover image is
Saint Augustine in His Study (1480) by Sandro Botticelli.
The text is set in 11/13 pt Arno Pro, a typeface
designed by Robert Slimbach.

To Professor Timothy Long,
whose knowledge, humor, and care
made learning a joy at a Providential time:

Ὡς μέγα το μικρόν ἐστιν ἐν καιρώ δοθέν.

CONTENTS

PREFACE ix

PROLOGUE 3

1 • Born and Raised in Africa 6
2 • Early Life 11
3 • Education, Rhetoric, and Teaching 15
4 • Manichaeism and Sexual Sin 20
5 • Ambrose 24
6 • Conversion 28
7 • The Pastorate at Hippo 35
8 • Life as Bishop: Heresies, Debates, Imperial Power 39
9 • Life as Bishop: Daily Life 47
10 • Life as Bishop: Writing and Preaching 51
11 • The Sack of Rome 55
12 • City of God 61
13 • Pelagianism 69
14 • Old Age 77
15 • Death and the End of Roman Hippo 86
16 • Legacy 92

APPENDIX A • Where to Go from Here? 99
APPENDIX B • Augustine and the Pears 105
APPENDIX C • Timeline of Important Events 110

PREFACE

AUGUSTINE is a man frequently encountered but seldom understood. If we run into his name at all, it's in passing. We may hear it in history class, or in church along with one of his many witty quotations, or even on vacation in Florida, in the city named after him.

I had met Augustine in all of those places, but mostly didn't notice. My first lasting encounter with him was in a first-year Latin course. On the board loomed a Latin sentence waiting to be translated. It was elegant and memorable, chosen (as Latin grammars are fond of doing) for its content *and* style. But unlike the many other sentences we had translated about sailors traveling, disembarking, and saving inhabitants from evil queens, this one was about friendship. And it was beautiful—that is, once our dear Professor Flaschenriem finally helped a struggling student translate it. But then, another student asked where it came from. Thinking a bit, she responded, "I think it's from Augustine." She'd heard he liked to write about friendship.

That moment was twenty-two years ago, and has till now lain dormant in my mind, but not for lack of exposure to Augustine. For at least fifteen years since then, through graduate school, through further study, and for the publication of this book, Augustine had been my focus. But none of those things unearthed this memory. What did so, rather, was remembering *why* I had studied Augustine in the first place: his *words*.

More words survive from Augustine than from any other

ancient author. During his long life, it was his words that gave rise to his career, thrilled his supporters, and roused his enemies. At the time of his death, it was his words that his fellow Christians strove mightily to safeguard and preserve. After his death, it was his words that ensured his longevity and endeared him to the ages. His words, more than anything, caused a profligate wanderer named Aurelius Augustine to become the revered "Saint Augustine."[1]

For even before his name received such honors, Augustine was a man of words. From his earliest days learning language, to his training and professorship in rhetoric, to his rescuing of rhetoric as a tool for Christian pastors, words are at the core of his being. But not just words for their own sake—rather, words for the sake of spiritual gain.

For God reveals Himself first in the incarnate Word, and then also in the words of Scripture. And this is key to any study of Augustine. As he worked through what sin had done to mankind, Augustine perceived a massive "dislocation" across humanity: man was now separated from God, and also separated from himself, his true emotions, his true self-understanding. Only the words of God could cross the divide and restore man to true knowledge and true feeling—that is, put him back together.

These are, clearly, huge issues. And throughout his life, Augustine approached them from different angles: sometimes as a philosopher, sometimes as a preacher, sometimes as a historian—but always as a Christian. In learning about him in this book, this will be our tack as well.

This book is diminutive by design. In its few pages there is time only to glimpse the colossal theology Augustine built, little room to discuss the network of friends he maintained, and barely any chance to understand his political theory. We will skim the surface of all of these, leaving the bulk of it to be investigated further by you, the reader.

---

1. There is a long (and appropriate) history of honoring Augustine with the title "Saint." Yet it also (especially for modern readers) can tend to distance him from our experience, and leave a misimpression of the nature of holiness and sin. Augustine would be the first to remind us that every "saint" was above all a sinner living in daily repentance. For these reasons, we will refer to him simply as "Augustine" and let his life and reputation speak for both his sins and his godliness.

After all, there are many possible Augustines to investigate: Augustine the wanderer, the son, the father, the bishop, the philosopher, the political and military theorist, the letter writer, even the physicist. But all of these are bound together by the experiences of Augustine's life, and how they taught him to be obsessed with knowing God, and knowing himself. If this slight book accomplishes no more than awakening in us a fragment of these things, it will have succeeded.

For this work, I have made a split decision about translations. For quotations from Augustine's *Confessions*, I have used the classic translation by J. G. Pilkington, with slight modernization. For all other ancient quotations the translations are mine,[2] unless otherwise noted. Places where writers themselves quote Scripture are indicated with the scriptural text in italics.

My gratitude is due to far too many to list here. Any biography of Augustine owes a great debt to Peter Brown's groundbreaking work, which opened up to me as to so many others the bishop of Hippo. There are, I'm sure, countless echoes in this text to events, approaches, and ideas first given voice in Brown's monumental work, and this is tribute to the imprint he has left on those of us who follow. Thanks also to Warhorn Media, Nathan Alberson, and especially Alex McNeilly for work in editing, proofreading, and publishing.

Most of all, I am indebted to my family. First, to my dad, who told me of Augustine long before I met him elsewhere. To my dear wife, whose patience in all areas has enabled this work to come to fruition. Having such a wife is one area where I have been more blessed by God than Augustine was! And finally, I am grateful for the children God's entrusted to us. In their joys and sorrows and sins I discover my own. And by their lives they teach us (as Augustine would ever remind us) both the corruption of their father Adam, and the splendor of the eternal Father of lights, from whom *every good and perfect gift cometh down from above* (James 1:17).

---

2. Such translations are taken from the latest critical text of each work, found in *Series Latina*, Corpus Christianorum (Turnhout: Brepols, 1953–) (*CCSL*).

BEHOLD
MY HEART

PROLOGUE

*I*N THE WINTER OF AD 429, a Roman soldier and diplomat named Count Darius received a letter from Augustine, the bishop of Hippo. Now some 75 years of age, and in failing health, the old bishop sent a number of letters in the final year of his life to Darius, who was at the center of the political and military crisis engulfing Roman Africa.

The situation in Augustine's land was grave. For five hundred years, it had been part of the Roman world, for better or worse. That world represented the greatest empire ever known, in territory that stretched from Britain to Spain, to Turkey, to Persia, and all of North Africa. But recently, things had changed. Roman power had begun to fall away before warrior tribes who smelled an opportunity. In the spring of 429, one of these tribes took their chance: the Vandals crossed the Straits of Gibraltar to attack the western borders of Roman Africa. Their force was some eighty thousand strong.

Against this onslaught, Roman defenses fell apart. Even the general charged to protect Roman Africa had, it seemed, betrayed his mission by making a truce with the enemy. This was the situation Augustine aimed to correct; he hoped that his letter to the diplomat Darius could convince him to reenlist the general's services to protect Africa from invasion.

It was not to be. From Gibraltar, the Vandal force swept

eastward across Africa. Though they claimed to be Christian,[1] their conduct was anything but. Towns, houses, and fields were burnt, women were raped, and children cut in two. Churches were pillaged, their congregations killed while worshiping, and their pastors and bishops slaughtered. Indeed, the Vandals seemed to save their greatest ire for clergymen and their churches. No bishop was exempt from the devastation, least of all Augustine, Africa's most prominent one. Even as his letter to Darius went out, his city of Hippo was besieged, and he would die before the siege ended—his city and the rest of Roman Africa falling to the Vandals.

Such was the situation when Darius received his letter from Augustine. The old bishop was no stranger to political and military negotiations, having operated for decades in behind-the-scenes maneuvers to persuade a supposedly Christian government to act that way. Though he had long held that the destiny of Rome did not coincide with that of Christianity, he still had tried to ensure that the structures of Rome protected the Church from enemies both spiritual and physical.

So it is surprising to find that, in his letter to Darius, there is almost no mention of any of this. Instead, Augustine's letter is a sunny recollection of the glories of friendship, love, and shared faith. Instead of urgent pleadings for aid, we find gentle greetings, warm assurances of friendship, and allusions to classic literature. And instead of requests for resources, we find Augustine offering a resource of his own: his autobiography *Confessions*, given unapologetically as an aid to the spiritual growth not only of Darius, but others also:

> Since you mentioned you have been aided by these labors [writings] of mine, ... shall I reckon it of small value how much benefit ... they might bring to others? ... Accept then, my son, accept, my good man—a Christian by Christian love rather than outward profession—accept, I say, the books you wished for, of my

---

1. The Vandals, like most of the "barbarian" tribes threatening Rome, were Arians, condemned in AD 325 as heretics by the Council of Nicaea because they denied that the Son was "of the same essence" as the Father.

Confessions . . . . And when you find me there, pray for me, that I may not fall short, but may be perfected. Pray, my son, pray. (*Letters* 231.5–6)

Needless to say, Augustine's choice of conversational topics here is odd. In the midst of catastrophe, why does Augustine only ask prayer for his own *spiritual* perseverance? Why does he spend time talking to Darius about the condition of his soul rather than his diplomatic efforts? And why does Augustine ask Darius to spend his time reading his autobiography? In a world about to be wasted by war, why dally with the pleasures of peace?

To answer these questions, we need to understand what events made Augustine the man he was. As we do so, we will find there is no better summary of his life than the one he gives to Darius, in what is perhaps his final letter:

Accept . . . the books . . . of my *Confessions*: there examine me, lest you praise me beyond what I am; there believe not others about me but me myself; there consider, and see what I have been in myself, through myself; and if anything in me pleases you, praise along with me there not me, but Him whom I have wanted to be praised on my account. *For He Himself made us, and not we ourselves*; indeed, we had destroyed ourselves, but he who made us, made us anew. (*Letters* 231.6)

1

Born and Raised in Africa

$\mathcal{A}$ugustine was born in AD 354 in the town of Thagaste, North Africa, in what is now Algeria. The region today is unfamiliar to most of us—and for good reason, as the Islamic conquest in the sixth century severed it from its classical history. We now think of it as Middle Eastern, but in Augustine's time, it was Roman.

North Africa was, in fact, a bastion of Roman rule in the midfourth century. Its residents had been Roman citizens for twice as long as today's Americans have belonged to the United States.

In Augustine's mind at least, the concept of living outside Rome's world was nearly inconceivable. Though his detractors might tease him about his African accent (they did so throughout his life), there was no doubt for them or him that he was Roman, through and through.

Augustine's Africa was the breadbasket of the Empire. Stretching up and down the coast of the Mediterranean were fields that fed the Roman world. For most of his life, the sight of these fields of grain and rows of olives would fill Augustine's mind, and in later days they would be the subjects of his sermons, ever ready to provide a needed metaphor or moral for Augustine's people. The realities of life and death, famine and fortune, were never far from view for the people of Augustine's world.

Augustine's Africa was also a conservative world. His hometown, Thagaste, was of no great importance, but it lay only a short distance from Carthage, a major metropolitan center. Thanks to the archaeologist's spade, we have a hint of the glories of this past world (long buried by the violence of the Vandal and Islamic invasions). Amphitheaters, circus tracks, marketplaces—all the glories of ancient civilization at its height were here for the viewing. Carthage was a reminder of the importance of Africa, as well as the legacy of ancient paganism in this now-Christian land.

Christianity had come to Africa some two hundred years before Augustine was born, and Africans embraced it with vigor. It was an African, Tertullian, who was likely the first Church Father to write in Latin. Africa was also known for Perpetua, the virgin whose unwillingness to recant her faith helped galvanize Christians for martyrdom. And then, in the generation before Augustine, Africa had been led by Cyprian, the bishop who lost his life in the large-scale persecution of the emperor Decius. In an increasingly Christian empire, Africans were known for being steadfast, practical, and maybe even obstinate.

But unlike with Christian Africa, "Christian" Rome was still a new thing in the mid-fourth century. It had only been forty years since the emperor Constantine had dramatically thrown his lot in with Christians, making Rome no longer their persecutor, but their protector. Still, since then, while Christianity had spread among the upper classes, allegiance to the old "gods" had proved hard to eradicate in rural, conservative areas.[1]

Converts to Christianity brought remnants of their pagan ways with them—later on, Augustine would (with some disapproval) speak of the gifts of food and wine that his mother was still bringing to graves of the martyrs! Old ways died hard in Africa.

The result was a population with both Christian and pagan elements, and nowhere was this truer than in Augustine's parents. His mother, Monica, was a Christian in both profession and life. When and how she became a Christian is unknown, but the intensity of her faith is felt everywhere in Augustine's writings. Patricius, Augustine's father, was a pagan.

---

1. Our word "pagan" comes from a term having the sense of "bumpkin," used pejoratively by *Christians* to highlight the old-fashionedness of their rivals.

Theirs was thus a mixed marriage, a situation not unusual for the time (particularly given how many Christians were women), but distressing to both her and her son. Reflecting on his mother's virtues as a wife, Augustine would later point out her wisdom in not opposing or quarreling with her husband when he was angry or drunk: submitting graciously to him, she was a noble example for other women.

Augustine was one of at least four children: we know of a brother Navigius, another unnamed brother, and an unnamed sister.[2] Otherwise, we hear little about his family life. Augustine's family seems to have been basically middle class. His father was a *decurio*, a member of the local government. He had connections to powerful people, yet seemed to have little power or wealth himself. Thus, for instance, while Augustine would benefit from a rhetorical education that few in Africa could hope for, his parents had to save every penny and use every connection to make it happen.

And yet his father's provision for his schooling is nearly the only praise Augustine can offer concerning him. In almost all of Augustine's recounting of his life, his father is absent. Augustine speaks of his violent temper, as mentioned above. We hear, too, in one painful passage from *Confessions*, that his father was overjoyed when he discovered his son had entered puberty, and so could offer him an heir. For a son longing for approval and spiritual direction, Patricius can offer only profane and worldly counsel, and this disappointment is evident whenever Augustine speaks of him. Indeed, there is a note of skepticism even in Augustine's recounting of his father's deathbed conversion—though Augustine asks his reader to thank God for both of his parents, we leave the passage pained at the missed spiritual opportunities Augustine must have regretted in his father's life.

Not so with his mother. If Augustine's autobiography *Confessions* is principally about his relationship with God as his Father, its secondary theme is his relationship with Monica, his mother.

---

2. We know little of her, except that later in life she was a widow and in charge of the "handmaidens of the Lord" at a convent in Hippo (Possidius, *Sancti Augustini Vita* [*Life of St. Augustine*] 26).

Warm, caring, and devoted, Monica could also be intense, fiery, even smothering. It is Monica who protects Augustine from his sometimes temperamental father, Monica who wants to see her son succeed in rhetorical school, and Monica who prays night and day for her wayward son to be converted to God.

Yet it is also Monica who turns Augustine out of her house because of his blasphemies,[3] Monica who refuses to allow him to marry his lower-class lover, and Monica who has to be told by her bishop to let Augustine be his own man, trusting that God will bring him out of falsehood. Like, perhaps, many men with intense, devoted mothers, Augustine's life was shaped by the faith, but also the failings, of his mother.

While Augustine mostly praises Monica, he is also not afraid to tell us her sins. There was her habit of bringing food and wine to the martyrs' graves. There is also implied criticism from her son that she did not have him baptized early on, in what Augustine thinks would have set him on the path of godliness and prevented his wanderings. Then too, Augustine expresses regret that his mother did not spare him the sins of lust by providing him a wife at an early age.

Yet even Augustine's criticisms are in the context of his desire to follow her faith. Indeed, most of his autobiography deals with the tension between the calls of his father's world (career, politics, etc.) and those of his mother's Church. Would it be worldly baubles that he would seek, or would it be the conversion of his soul and life in the Church his mother served so devotedly?

As we shall see, the latter eventually triumphed in Augustine's life, yet the road was anything but straightforward. So it is appropriate that Augustine would save some of his most poignant writing in *Confessions* for a final exchange he had with his mother *after* his conversion. After so many tears, she had finally seen her heart's desire accomplished by God, and, in her words, could now die. Soon after, she did just that. As is typical, Augustine's words are both eulogy and prayer to God:

---

3. *Confessions* 3.11.19.

I then, O my Praise and my Life, God of my heart, putting aside for a little her good deeds, for which I joyfully give thanks to You, do now beseech You for the sins of my mother.... Let Your mercy be exalted above Your justice, because Your words are true, and You have promised mercy unto the merciful...

May she therefore rest in peace with her husband, before or after whom she married none; whom she obeyed, with patience bringing forth fruit unto You, that she might gain him also for You. And inspire, O my Lord my God, inspire Your servants my brethren, Your sons my masters, who with voice and heart and writings I serve, that so many of them as shall read these confessions may at Your altar remember Monica, Your handmaid, together with Patricius, her sometime husband, by whose flesh You introduced me into this life, in what manner I know not. May they with pious affection be mindful of my parents in this transitory light, of my brethren that are under You our Father in our Catholic mother, and of my fellow citizens in the eternal Jerusalem. (*Confessions* 9.13.35, 9.13.37)

2

Early Life

*B*ECAUSE OF THE SHEER VOLUME OF HIS WRITINGS, and particularly because of the intimacy of *Confessions*, Augustine lets us peer into his soul in a way unrivaled in any author before the twentieth century. We should keep in mind that the glimpse he gives us is one of his choosing, and one that omits many aspects that Augustine felt unimportant or unworthy. Thus we learn little about any of Augustine's family except his mother, but learn a great deal about, say, his views on how children learn language!

Still, the depth of self-examination in Augustine's works is remarkable, as well as characteristic throughout his life. It pops to the surface early on in *Confessions*, where Augustine ponders for line after line where he may find God, and how his own soul can possibly see, hear, or interact with Him.

As he contemplates God's greatness and power in the created world, so he also traces how his own soul reacts to God and His commands. *Confessions* is, in one sense, nothing more than the account of the soul's journey from emptiness to fullness, from wanderings to home.

But this introspection is not an end in itself. It leads outward, to a sensitivity to the people and world around him. No man or thing in Augustine's experience is excluded from the intense curiosity of Augustine's gaze. Early on in *Confessions*, after focusing on his life as an infant, and how he communicated to his parents and nurses with non-verbal sign language, Augustine is led to consider other infants he has observed. Invariably, he recalls, they show the same envy that marks man in general. For example, do they not covet the breast even when others are already drinking from it? Do they not seek only their own desires, with no concern for others? Never before and hardly since has any author meditated on the inner lives of infants with such piercing analysis.

As Augustine grows, so does this sensitivity to the evil he finds in his own heart. Book 2 of *Confessions* brings him into adolescence, and with this, raises the ante considerably for the wickedness Augustine sees in himself. With puberty, Augustine finds himself in the grip of sexual desire, in the lust that will later appear throughout his writings as "concupiscence." Here, Augustine depicts it as more experimental, but nonetheless evil. The language Augustine uses to describe his predicament is vivid:

> There was no proper restraint, as in the union of mind with mind, where a bright boundary regulates friendship. From the mud of my fleshly desires and my erupting puberty belched out murky clouds that obscured and darkened my heart until I could not distinguish the calm light of love from the fog of lust. The two swirled about together and dragged me, young and weak as I was, over the cliffs of my desires, and engulfed me in a whirlpool of sins. (*Confessions* 2.2.2[1])

Augustine's parents were not caught unaware by their son's difficulties. Yet their reactions were, in Augustine's hindsight, too little, too late. From his nonbelieving father, Augustine's adolescent stirrings prompt only fatherly pride at the prospect of a future heir. His mother, by contrast, has plenty of negative advice to offer, but the young Augustine finds it of little value. Her words, though from God, seem to him merely a mother's chiding:

> And whose words were they but Yours which by my mother, Your faithful handmaid, You poured into my ears, none of which sank

[1]. Trans. Maria Boulding, *The Works of Saint Augustine: A Translation for the 21st Century*, pt. 1, vol. 1 (New City Press, 1997).

into my heart to make me do it? For she desired, and I remember privately warned me, with great solicitude, "not to commit fornication—but above all things never to defile another man's wife." These appeared to me but womanish counsels, which I should blush to obey. (*Confessions* 2.3.7)

Though she warned sternly against immorality, his mother apparently did little to find Augustine a wife for quite some time, a fact Augustine later faults her for.

But Augustine knows he is not a victim and that the origin of his sin cannot be located outside of himself. Rather, the lust he experiences is rooted in his soul, in a desire for love and satisfaction outside of God Himself. In Augustine's words, his desire was "only to love and to be loved." This awareness, that his heart desired fulfillment *outside of* God, is for Augustine characteristic of sin at its core. Sin deceives, demands, corrupts, and consumes. It presents itself as a *means* to external pleasure, but it actually demands that a man love the sin *itself*.

One of the most famous accounts from *Confessions* illustrates this point. Outside of his family's vineyard was a pear tree that he and his companions came upon late one night. Stripping the tree of its fruit, the band of thieves (as Augustine calls them) did so only to throw their pilferings to the swine. For Augustine, the theft was not the worst of his sin. Rather, his guilt lay in the fact that he picked the pears not because of poverty, nor from hunger, nor even for enjoyment, but simply to commit the sin itself. It was the sin itself that Augustine loved, and not the fruit of it:

> Behold my heart, O my God; behold my heart, which You had pity upon when in the bottomless pit. Behold, now, let my heart tell You what it was seeking there, that I should be gratuitously evil, having no inducement to evil but the evil itself. It was foul, and I loved it. I loved to perish. I loved my own error—not that for which I erred, but the error itself. (*Confessions* 2.4.9)[2]

---

2. For a fuller excerpt of the pear story as it appears in *Confessions*, see Appendix B.

The pear story also shows us that sin has a social aspect. All his life, Augustine treasured his friends, yet here, he finds in friendship a dark potential for magnifying the evil of the heart. This passage is one of the key passages about "peer pressure" that we find in the ancient world. But crucially, once again, Augustine is not content to find in his friends the root cause of his desire for theft:

> Yet alone I would not have done it—alone I could not at all have done it. Behold, my God, the lively recollection of my soul is laid bare before You—alone I would not have committed that theft, in which what I stole pleased me not, but rather the act of stealing; nor to have done it alone would I have liked so well, neither would I have done it. (*Confessions* 2.9.17)

The companions were the instrument that aroused the sin, but the sin resided deep in his own heart.

3

Education, Rhetoric, and Teaching

To understand Augustine and his world, we must understand education in his time, and in particular the study of rhetoric. For Augustine is, from first days to last, a rhetorician at heart. He is a word lover and a word wielder, a man who can devote thousands of words to the meaning of one (as he does in *Confessions*), or create stunning arrangements of words in expressing his love of Jesus Christ.

Education in Augustine's day centered on three elements: grammar, logic, and rhetoric. Grammar included all aspects of training in the mechanics and structure of language. Students would learn how to speak and write a language (both Greek and Latin), but would also be trained in principles of etymology, syntax, and so on. Logic (or "dialectic") encompassed using reason to guide one's thinking into rational paths—arguments, defenses, contradictions, and so on. Finally, rhetoric involved the art of persuasion in both written and oral forms—using the tools of grammar and logic to convince others.

We have to remember that education in the ancient world was bound up with speech and sound. A man did not "argue" with another over the privacy of email, chat, or even (usually) a written letter: he argued in public, with the spoken word, and often with an audience. (In that way, it somewhat resembles social media today, except that the focus was entirely oral, not written.) A student did not prepare an assignment to be handed in and graded by a teacher privately, but rather displayed his work in front of other students orally—reciting his verb conjugations, repeating a literary passage from memory, or participating in an argument with another student. Even reading was different from how we conceive of it today. It was done out loud, and books were written with this reality in mind. Indeed, Augustine tells us in his *Confessions* how shocked he was the first time he saw his bishop, Ambrose, reading Scripture without speaking. Reading, as with all other aspects of education, was a *public* activity.

Ancient rhetoric focused as much on *how* a sentence was communicated as on *what* it communicated. The purpose of writing was to persuade a reader or hearer by making the thought penetrate, resonate, and remain in his mind. (The surviving authors of antiquity are famous not just for the brilliance of their ideas but for the power of their styles.) A man who could dress up mediocre ideas with verbal elegance had a leg up on one whose more compelling ideas remained bare and plain.

Along with this emphasis on style came significant demands on the memory. In our time, when our houses are filled with unread books we can pick up for pennies, it is hard to conceive of how precious were books in the days before the printing press. Only the rich and well educated (a small minority) could either read or afford books, and this meant that the memory shouldered much more of the weight of education. Students performed their lessons through memorization; parishioners learned Scripture by hearing it read, sung, and preached; and orators and lawyers depended entirely on memory as they went about their work. Indeed, Augustine tells us in *Confessions* (1.1.3) that he was required to memorize the *Aeneid* (the great epic of Roman literature, running to some ten thousand lines) as a student. There is no indication from Augustine that this was uncommon or extraordinary!

This, then, was the system that nourished Augustine throughout his education, from his first years in his hometown of Thagaste, to his later training in the Roman city of Carthage. Such training was neither automatic nor cheap for a boy growing up in a middle-class family in Africa. Augustine's parents sacrificed a great deal for their son's education, but more was needed for Augustine to have a chance to make a good future in law or politics.

That help arrived in the person of Romanianus, a well-to-do acquaintance of Augustine's family. Romanianus became a patron supporter of Augustine, providing money and connections to enable him to continue his schooling. In return, Augustine was likely expected to use his talents to support the work and position of his patron.

Augustine was brilliant, but also undisciplined and distracted, as he admits in reflection. We have already seen this play out in the infamous pear story, which came about while Augustine was away from schooling for a year (while his father saved more money for his son's education). These distractions grew even more intense when, at age 17, Augustine transferred to the capital, Carthage, to finish his studies. Here was every kind of temptation. While in Carthage, Augustine spent time at the theater (whose allures were as bad or worse than in our time), hung out with a rowdy crowd of students calling themselves "the wreckers," and ignored his mother's advice by taking up with a woman.

In the midst of this "cauldron of illicit loves" (*Confessions* 3.1.1), Augustine found philosophy. He had met it before, of course, as philosophical texts were a cornerstone of Roman education. But somehow, this time it was different. Reading Cicero's (now lost) work *Hortensius* awakened in the young man a hunger for true meaning, true wisdom. Up to this point, Augustine's career path had aimed toward legal study, serving in the bureaucracy of the Empire, but now, this was not enough. Scrapping this plan, Augustine turned toward philosophical study. Perhaps it could give him a career and life with purpose. Perhaps this could make sense of the dissolute life he found himself in, and bring discipline to it. For the *Hortensius* warned against fleshly pleasures, and stressed intellectual discipline. Augustine knew this was right, and rejoiced with its goal—but could not accomplish it. Brilliant as he was, he was finding that neither education nor philosophy could bring the discipline, virtue, and purity he needed.

Three years passed. His studies in Carthage came to an end, and Augustine returned in 374 to his hometown to teach. His father had by this time passed away, and it may be that Augustine now felt it was time to establish a career in earnest. Soon after moving back, though, a close friend of Augustine's (he doesn't tell us his name) passed away. Living in his hometown, surrounded by memories, now became intolerable to Augustine, so he moved back to Carthage in 376, this time as a teacher.

Perhaps through the connections of his patron Romanianus, he soon found a professorship in Rome. For a middle-class African boy, to teach rhetoric in Rome was a dream come true. For a thousand years, Rome had been the center of Latin learning across the world. It was the city of Cicero, Augustine's newfound love. It was the city that had made (and broken) a thousand careers in law, politics, and rhetoric, and though it was no longer the official center of government (this had been moved to Ravenna), it had all of the panache and prestige that might be expected for a city called "eternal."

Yet, Augustine was not happy. The students he tried to teach were exasperating: they were mischievous pranksters and cheaters. Most distressing, many of them refused to pay their school bills, and Augustine soon grew disgusted with the lack of integrity in the rhetorical school. To make matters worse, he fell sick for an extended period of time. All in all, Rome was hardly the career pinnacle he had hoped for.

In Rome, however, was a pagan official who would alter the course of Augustine's life forever. Symmachus was his name, and his position as prefect of Rome meant he had connections higher than Augustine ever imagined: to the emperor of the Empire himself. It was Symmachus's responsibility to appoint a new chair of rhetoric in Milan, the city where the emperor was currently residing. The position was part professorship and part public spokesman for the emperor. By all rights, it was a position for a nobleman of Rome, not a middle-class African boy derided for his accent. But Symmachus had heard a speech Augustine had given in Rome, and soon after made his choice. The 30-year-old

Augustine of Africa would now become the chair of rhetoric in Milan.

Milan was the final destination in Augustine's rise to secular prominence, and yet also the apex of his unhappiness. In part, this was a consequence of his growing suspicion of the rhetoric that had made his name. Men used words of great brilliance and beauty, but seemed less concerned for the moral principles of their arguments. Beyond this, Augustine also was experiencing a religious crisis. In Milan, he would soon come face to face with Bishop Ambrose, the famous Christian bishop who had a reputation for both brilliance and boldness. Yet Augustine, though raised by a Catholic mother, had rejected the Church. His life for the past decade had in fact not been devoted to that Church, but rather to a curious philosophy that was a competitor to Christianity. That philosophy was Manichaeism.

4

Manichaeism and Sexual Sin

*T*HE RELIGIOUS WORLD OF AUGUSTINE'S TIME was, like ours today, in flux. Christianity, which had grown slowly but surely over the first three centuries after Christ's resurrection, had grown in prominence since Constantine's embrace of it some seventy-five years previous, and soon the emperor Theodosius would officially close all the pagan temples of the Empire. The writing was on the wall for Greco-Roman paganism.

Yet the old ways were slow to die in enclaves throughout the Empire. Not only that, but the ancient world was also awash with "variants" of Christianity constantly springing up. The Catholic (from a Greek term meaning "universal") Church had at the council of Nicaea (and elsewhere) upheld and declared what doctrine qualified as orthodox, as "right thinking," but non-orthodox sects of Christianity, and mixtures with pagan philosophy, were strewn throughout the world.

One of these was the philosophy that ensnared Augustine from age 18 until he was almost 30. It owed its name to Mani, a Persian "prophet" whose teachings are, to modern ears, often difficult to understand. Essentially, Manichaeism held that the universe was the site of a cosmic, eternal struggle between two opposing forces of good and evil. Elements of the good, divine principle were present in each man, yet imprisoned in the fleshly body. By discerning the truths that Mani proclaimed, and (for the higher-level followers) by renouncing physical pleasures, a Manichaean disciple could hope to free these forces of good within himself, so that they could be reunited and once again become part of deity. Manichaeism thus had the advantage of being exotic enough to attract jaded pagans, Christian enough for those wanting to claim that label, and immaterial enough for those who could not accept the physicality of the Bible.

For Augustine, these qualities made Manichaeism hard to resist. Having grown up in proximity to the Church, he maintained a certain respect for it and its Scripture, yet he recoiled from the sheer physicality of the Old Testament: sex, polygamous patriarchs and kings, blood, violence, uncouth prophets, and so on. In this, he was not alone: in the ancient world, the scandal of Scripture was not so much its call to "seek the things above" by following God, but rather its claim that God *had become man* by coming to earth. Today, living in a world filled with food, drink, sex, medicine, and so on, it is hard to imagine a time where *renouncing* these things was the way to popularity and glory. Yet this was Augustine's time in a nutshell, and it soured Augustine on much of Scripture.

Manichaeism, however, had no such problem, with its emphasis on the "spiritual." Ironically, it could glorify spiritual pursuits while at the same time allowing fleshly physical indulgence as inconsequential. Its stark dualistic system separated a man's physical actions from his spirit and soul, so that he could legitimately claim that that he himself had not committed a sin, but rather the dark forces within himself. For a man such as Augustine, whose mind struggled to understand the bondage of his soul, it was an appealing solution. He himself had not done the sin, but was captive to the dark, material prison in which the "light" had been trapped:

> It still seemed to me "that it was not we that sin, but [some other nature] sinned in us." And it gratified my pride to be free from blame and, after I had committed any fault, not to acknowledge that I had done any.... I loved to excuse it, and to accuse something else ... which was with me, but was not I. But assuredly it was wholly I, and my impiety had divided me against myself; and

that sin was all the more incurable in that I did not deem myself a sinner. (*Confessions* 5.10.18)

Augustine had struggled all his life to explain the problem of evil. Where did evil come from, and how could we account for it in ourselves? By relegating his sin outside of himself, Augustine now felt he had a solution.

As time went on, however, this Manichaean sleight of hand became less tolerable for Augustine. Desiring to understand more about the system, he sought out the assistance of Faustus, a famous Manichaean bishop. The meeting was momentously disappointing. Far from assuaging Augustine's concerns, Faustus was incapable of answering his questions and objections. Augustine remained a Manichaean, but a doubtful one, and unable to rid himself of sin.

For some specially motivated Manichaeans (termed "the elect" by Mani), a higher level of attainment beckoned, but required severe ascetic renunciation. The elect would need to give up meat, wine, possession of property, and, most important for Augustine, sexual activity.

This was the pressing issue for Augustine, and had been for many years. Having spurned his mother's "womanly" counsel towards purity, he had found himself unable to be chaste, yet also unable to approve of his sin. "Give me chastity, but not yet" is his familiar cry in *Confessions*, wanting to be set free, but unable to be so (8.7.17).

Yet for all his inability to be chaste, his affections did, it seems, settle on one woman—the lover mentioned earlier, with whom he took up in Carthage. We know almost nothing of her—Augustine does not even tell us her name. To her, however, Augustine says he was faithful—and we know that, when Augustine was about 18, she gave him a son. Adeodatus ("Gift of God") was his name, and for a time, Augustine, though formally unmarried, could at least claim a sort of common-law marriage and family.

It was not to last. In 385, Monica finally (recall Augustine's earlier complaint) arranged a suitable marriage for her son. But the woman she chose would not be Augustine's lover, with whom he already had a son. Why? The answer likely has much to do with the social realities of marriage in late Roman society. Augustine's lover was almost certainly of a lower class, and thus an impossible choice for him to marry. And so the plans for Augustine's marriage moved forward, with one small yet painful detail: the bride's parents had mandated that Augustine be separated from his lover for at least two years before the wedding. This longstanding relationship now ended forever.

Augustine was heartbroken. The woman he had known and loved for fourteen years, and the mother of his son, was now torn from them both. Never denying the sinfulness of his relations, Augustine in hindsight nonetheless leaves the reader with some of the most emotionally wrenching words in all of his writings:

> Meanwhile my sins were being multiplied, and my mistress being torn from my side as an impediment to my marriage, my heart, which clave to her, was racked, and wounded, and bleeding. And she went back to Africa, making a vow unto You never to know another man, leaving with me my natural son by her. (*Confessions* 6.15.25)

Of this woman Augustine never speaks again in any of his writings. Whether from shame, guilt, love, or pain, he is silent. He had been faithful to her in the midst of his immorality, yet now, with no prospect of a relationship for some two years, he again finds chastity impossible, and takes another woman to satisfy his desires.

This, then, is the state of Augustine's life in Milan. Disillusioned with teaching, it has nonetheless brought him to the heart of Roman power. A Manichaean for some twelve years, he is now fed up with its strange and irrational explanations of reality. And, though emotionally devastated by his sin with the woman he loved, he cannot rid himself of his need to be loved. He is, in short, a man who has both gained and lost nearly everything. But in Milan is more than just a career; in it is Augustine's spiritual future, from a man who will make that future his mission. In Milan, is Bishop Ambrose.

5

Ambrose

For students of church history, Bishop Ambrose is second only to Augustine among the late Church Fathers in the influence he exerted on future generations. His breeding, political savvy, and faith masked the fact that he was, in fact, only ten years older than Augustine. Born into a well-to-do Roman Christian family, he had studied the best of law, philosophy, and politics. His career had advanced quickly, and in 372 he became a Roman governor at age 28 in provinces that included the city of Milan. Such a position, in a city as prominent as Milan, brought him both power and popularity.

Yet, as was true with his protégé Augustine, God had other ideas. In the late fourth century, the Church was full of strife on the matter of Christology. Though the doctrine championed by Athanasius (d. 373) held that the Son of God was coequal with God the Father, the Arians disputed this. For over fifty years the controversy had continued, and was still hot in Ambrose's time in Milan.

In 374, Ambrose waded into the dispute. The bishop of Milan had just died, and the question of who would succeed him threatened to send Milan into turmoil. But upon addressing the crowd, Ambrose suddenly found himself interrupted with cries of "Ambrose, bishop!" Ambrose was unprepared for such an office, and so at first rejected the idea, but gave in when the emperor of Rome threw his weight behind the popular acclaim.

Ambrose's appointment signaled the rise of a new generation of churchmen committed to Catholic doctrine. Educated at the highest levels, he brought the richness of his training to bear in his new work, in both scriptural study and in preaching. Cicero and Plato now met Moses and Paul.

Equally important, it turned out, was Ambrose's past life in Roman politics. As the son of a Roman official, and as a former governor himself, Ambrose had an uncanny understanding for how the imperial machinery worked. The result of this political savvy was that, more than any other church official, Ambrose knew how to manipulate levers of power to accomplish the work of the Church.

We see this in his confrontation of the emperor Theodosius in 390. The emperor had recently ordered a massacre of seven thousand people in Thessalonica, in retribution for the murder of the Roman governor there. As John the Baptist had done four centuries earlier, the Church now confronted the civil authority, condemning the highest sovereign in the land, and requiring repentance. Indeed, as proof of the latter, Ambrose demanded that Theodosius display public penance for several months before he would readmit him to the Lord's Supper—and the emperor obeyed. The sight of a Roman emperor publicly removing his royal clothing and bowing to a bishop was not soon forgotten in the Roman world.

And there was more. Soon after Augustine's arrival in Milan, the Western emperor Valentinian (who was an Arian) demanded that Ambrose give over a Milanese Catholic church for use by the Arians. Ambrose, who had taken a hard line against Arianism, refused. The empress mother, Justina, then sent imperial troops to the church to force Ambrose's cooperation. But Ambrose remained unfazed, refusing entry to the Arians, and sealing himself and the congregation in the church. It was a moment for the ages: a Roman garrison threatening to destroy a church with the bishop and former governor within, while meanwhile that bishop led his congregation in singing hymns to pass the time and lift their spirits. Years later, Augustine would write about the incident, remembering his mother's joy and confidence in Ambrose's decisions. Eventually, Justina and Valentinian backed down. Ambrose had called their bluff, showing that imperial might no longer trumped the authority of the Church.

But for Augustine, none of these things mattered as much as one thing: Ambrose's preaching. Augustine had met faithful Christians before, most of all his mother. He had also seen sophistication and power. What Augustine had *not* met before was anyone with such power and brilliance who preached the orthodox Christian faith. Ambrose's preaching was of a type Augustine had never before heard: learned, and yet not embarrassed to confess the simple truths of the faith. While Augustine had always shunned the Old Testament and its earthy accounts, Ambrose handled them with aplomb, revealing the spiritual and allegorical meaning of even the thorniest text. Under Ambrose, Augustine found his objections to Scripture melting away. Increasingly, he found that Scripture and logic need not be at odds with each other.

One tool used by Ambrose was especially effective in convincing Augustine. This was Neoplatonism, a descendant of the ideas taught by Plato some eight centuries earlier. Like many Christians, Ambrose took some of its precepts and used them to help unravel difficult sections of Scripture. By emphasizing the spiritual significance of everyday, vulgar descriptions, Ambrose could show that the Old Testament was not to be shunned by serious Christians.

Augustine felt some of the blinders finally coming off. Here was a philosophy that, unlike Manichaeism, needed no bizarre concepts to explain reality. Here was a system that, to a mind trained in classical logic and rhetoric, brought Scripture's teaching into clear focus. And here was a teaching that showed in vivid detail Augustine's need to forsake the fleshly desires holding him back, and seek the things that were above. For Augustine, reading the books of the Neoplatonists was no less than a revelation to him, brought by God to bring him closer to Jesus Christ.

It may seem strange to us in hindsight that Augustine would link so closely the work of pagan philosophers to the awakening of his faith in Christ, yet this is precisely what he does. Indeed, long after his conversion Augustine's writings are still marked by an affinity for Platonic ideas. At the same time, he realizes the limitations of the Platonists:

> In like manner, I read there that God the Word was born not of flesh, nor of blood, nor of the will of man, nor of the will of the flesh, but of God. But that *the Word was made flesh, and dwelt among us*, I read not there. (*Confessions* 7.9.14)

The Platonists thus had shown Augustine the problem, but could not provide the final solution. For his part, Ambrose had removed for Augustine the intellectual obstacles to belief, but to share fully in Ambrose's faith, Augustine needed more than intellectual enlightenment. He needed, as he would say, conversion of the heart.

6

Conversion

By the year 386, Augustine was 32 years old, at the height of his career as a public spokesman for the emperor, and on the verge of a proper Roman marriage. His mother Monica and son Adeodatus now lived with him (and possibly a brother, Navigius, as well), and he had a slew of friends around him whom he engaged on questions of philosophy and religion. Even his concerns about Christianity's intellectual claims had found solid answers under Bishop Ambrose, whose instruction had been the tool to open Augustine's eyes to Scripture. Yet as we read about this part of his life in book 8 of *Confessions*, what is striking is how unsatisfied Augustine still was.

Then one day an imperial official named Ponticianus came to visit. Seeing a copy of the Apostle Paul's letters that Augustine had been reading, Ponticianus spoke about his own spiritual testimony, and in the process spoke of the experiences of Anthony of Egypt (d. 356). Visiting a church one day, Anthony had entered just in time to hear Christ's words from Matthew 19:21: "Sell what you have and give to the poor, and you will have treasure in heaven; and come, follow Me." He was certain it was a command meant for him, and so he founded a monastery where he and his colleagues lived ascetic lives devoted to prayer. Referring to this account, Ponticianus then explained how two of his own colleagues had themselves renounced their careers and followed the same path.

Ponticianus's words stirred a fire within Augustine to follow the model of Anthony. Having finally put to rest the Manichaean objections, Augustine was now ready for a life devoted to following Christ. Career, money, family, and fame—all these he was willing to give up in exchange for a life entirely focused on serving God.

But one obstacle remained: chastity. Since adolescence, this had been the area that had defied all attempts at control, and Augustine had not been able to conceive of his life without the embraces of a woman:

> While I talked of these things, and these winds veered about and tossed my heart here and there, the time passed on; but I was slow to turn to the Lord, and from day to day deferred to live in You, and deferred not daily to die in myself. Being enamored of a happy life, I yet feared it in its own abode, and, fleeing from it, sought after it. I conceived that I should be too unhappy were I deprived of the embraces of a woman; and of Your merciful medicine to cure that infirmity I thought not, not having tried it. (*Confessions* 6.11.20)

At this point, we might ask why a decision to convert to Christianity required a vow of celibacy for Augustine. No such vow was in general practice, either in Scripture or in the Christianity of his time. Even clergy and bishops were not forbidden from marriage,[1] still less a layman such as Augustine. And had not the Apostle Paul explicitly counseled that it was "better to marry than to burn"?

Augustine never fully explains his reasoning on this, but it's clear from his own words that, for him personally, Christianity, chastity, and celibacy were inseparable. Perhaps Augustine's own experience of his parents' marriage inclined him to think of marriage as an impediment to spiritual growth. Perhaps the example

---

1. Clerical celibacy grew gradually over the centuries, first as custom, and then finally as mandatory church law in the twelfth century. In Augustine's time, general practice was increasingly favoring some kind of celibacy: at first, that married clergy not engage in sexual relations, and later, that clergy not be married at all.

of Ambrose, Augustine's spiritual father, led him to remain unmarried.[2] Perhaps the prospect of giving up career and property were incompatible with supporting a wife and family. Or, it may simply be that Augustine's long and taxing history with immorality meant that he could not imagine sexual relations in a holy context.

Whatever the reason, there is no hint in Augustine's writings that he ever considered marriage and Christianity as compatible in his own life. It was all or nothing for Augustine. Having heard from Ponticianus about the renunciation of his two colleagues, Augustine exclaimed to his lifelong friend Alypius in a moment of grief:

> What is wrong with us? What is this? What did you hear? The unlearned start up and "take" heaven, and we, with our learning, but wanting heart, see where we wallow in flesh and blood! Because others have preceded us, are we ashamed to follow, and not rather ashamed at not following? (*Confessions* 8.8.19)

Stirred by these thoughts and the realization of his own sin, Augustine retired with Alypius to the garden of the house. And here, he meditated, and prayed, and agonized, and wept. For hours, perhaps. Torn between the call of Christ and the call of his flesh, he heard himself crying, "Let it be done now, let it be done now." But then, whispering in his ears, he heard the voice of all his allurements, saying, "Are you going to really get rid of us? Do you think you can live without us?" Finally, from the other side, a vision of Continence personified beckoned to him:

> She smiled on me with an encouraging mockery, as if to say, "Can you not do what these youths and maidens can? Or can one or other do it of themselves, and not rather in the Lord their God? The Lord their God gave me unto them. Why do you stand in your own strength, and so stand not? Cast yourself upon Him; fear not, He will not withdraw that you should fall; cast yourself

---

2. Ambrose had also written against clergy having children (Ambrose, *Letters* 63.62), which may have influenced Augustine.

upon Him without fear, He will receive you, and heal you." (*Confessions* 8.11.27)

Finally, unable to do what his heart longed for, Augustine burst into sobbing, and cast himself down under a fig tree. Suddenly, he heard from a distance the voice of a child chanting, "Take up and read; take up and read." Deciding that the voice was not that of a child playing, but rather a sign from heaven, he returned to the texts he had been reading, and read the first paragraph his eyes came upon: "Not in revelry and drunkenness, not in lewdness and lust, not in strife and envy. But put on the Lord Jesus Christ, and make no provision for the flesh, to fulfill its lusts" (Rom. 13:13b–14).

Instantly, all the doubt fell away from his soul. Returning to Alypius, he found that his friend had been experiencing much the same. Alypius asked Augustine what he had been reading, and then himself read the very next verse: "Him that is weak in the faith, receive," a verse Alypius immediately applied to himself. Their hearts now at rest, they immediately told Monica, who was overjoyed at the news.

So it was that, by an off-chance visit of an imperial official, and the unknown chanting of a child, Augustine was converted to Christ. He now resigned his position of service to the emperor. He canceled the engagement Monica had arranged for him. And in the six months or so that would precede his baptism, Augustine and some of his friends withdrew to a small country villa in the Roman town of Cassiciacum. Here, Augustine established a life much like the dream he had always had—a life centered around study of the liberal arts, where like-minded men would "retire" to contemplate the truths of creation. But now, this dream would have a distinctively Christian vision, as he and his burgeoning Christian community would seek, together, to pursue God through study of Scripture and philosophy. As a man who never wanted to be alone, Augustine now had a critical mass of family and friends: his mother, his son, his brother, and at least two other friends (Alypius, Nebridius), all unified in their pursuit of the riches of Christian truth.

On Easter Sunday of 387, Augustine, his son Adeodatus, and his friend Alypius were all baptized by Bishop Ambrose in Milan. The prayers and tears of his mother had found favor with God, as her son's course was changed forever at the age of 33. And, with his plans finally set, Augustine now decided to return home to Thagaste.

But things would soon change. The stability Augustine thought he had achieved would not last. For one, the political situation in Europe had become tumultuous, and for several months, a military blockade kept Augustine and his party in Italy. The delay was undoubtedly frustrating, yet it had the benefit of allowing Augustine and his mother to reconnect, now with a shared faith. In a passage that is both mysterious and compelling, Augustine tells of the glories of God that he and his mother experienced together:

> And when our conversation had arrived at that point, . . . we . . . gradually passed through all corporeal things, and even the heaven itself, whence sun, and moon, and stars shine upon the earth; yea, we soared higher yet by inward musing, and discoursing, and admiring Your works; and we came to our own minds, and went beyond them, that we might advance as high as that region of unfailing plenty, where You feed Israel for ever with the food of truth, and where life is that Wisdom by whom all these things are made. (*Confessions* 9.10.24)

This experience is perhaps the most joyous one Augustine ever relates. Augustine's mother told him that her life's wishes had now come true. And now that he had become a Christian, there was little else for her in life. And so, some five days later, his mother died. Augustine was devastated, yet not inconsolable. He remembered the courage and Christian faith with which his mother faced death, even how she was unafraid to be buried far away from her husband in a foreign land:

> I heard afterwards, too, . . . when they . . . asked her whether she did not dread leaving her body at such a distance from her own

city, she replied, "Nothing is far to God; nor need I fear lest He should be ignorant at the end of the world of the place whence He is to raise me up." (*Confessions* 9.11.28)

As is typical with Augustine, his recounting of his own grief is not simply inwardly focused, but also has an external purpose—to show how a Christian both should and should not grieve:

> I closed her eyes; and there flowed a great sadness into my heart, and it was passing into tears, when my eyes at the same time, by the violent control of my mind, sucked back the fountain dry, and woe was me in such a struggle! But, as soon as she breathed her last the boy Adeodatus burst out into wailing, but, being checked by us all, he became quiet. In like manner also my own childish feeling, which was, through the youthful voice of my heart, finding escape in tears, was restrained and silenced. For we did not consider it fitting to celebrate that funeral with tearful plaints and groanings; for this is often the way those who die unhappy, or are altogether dead, are mourned. But she neither died unhappy, nor did she altogether die....
>
> So, when the body was carried forth, we both went and returned without tears.... yet was I most grievously sad in secret all the day, and with a troubled mind entreated You, as I was able, to heal my sorrow...
>
> And then little by little did I bring back my former thoughts of Your handmaid, her devout conversation towards You, her holy tenderness and attentiveness towards us, which was suddenly taken away from me; and it was pleasant to me to weep in Your sight, for her and for me, concerning her and concerning myself. ... Let whoever wishes read it, and interpret as he will; and if he finds me to have sinned in weeping for my mother during so small a part of an hour—that mother who was for a while dead to my eyes, who had for many years wept for me, that I might live in Your eyes—let him not laugh at me, but rather, if he be a man of a noble charity, let him weep for my sins against You, the Father of all the brethren of Your Christ. (*Confessions* 9.12.29–33)

His mother buried, Augustine and his party finally returned to Africa the next summer. He settled his property, established his monastic community, and prepared to live the life he had planned before the loss of his mother.

Yet sorrow was not done with him. Soon after returning to Africa, his friend Nebridius died, for reasons that are unknown to us. And, worst of all, in the year 388, Augustine lost his only son Adeodatus. He was 17. Unlike with Monica, Augustine tells us almost nothing of the loss of his son. We may suspect that, to Augustine, Adeodatus remained all his life a source of both great pride and also lingering grief—pride in the brilliance and sensitivity we learn of him from Augustine's works, but also grief in his connection to Augustine's ten-year sexual sin. Was this the reason for Augustine's silence on the death of his only son? Was it because he was a reminder of the woman Augustine loved more than any other? Or was it because Augustine simply couldn't bring himself to put into words the loss of his only son? We simply do not know.

And so, by the age of 35, Augustine had lost his father, mother, common-law wife, friend, and only son. He had left behind his career, his status, his fame, and his rhetoric. And he had disposed of all his property. What he had gained, however, was far greater, and Augustine would ever have us remember this. For he had gained God the Father Almighty, the final peace of his own soul, and the service of His Church. Such service he thought would be in quiet retirement, but God would show him something quite different. Far from retirement, the next forty years of Augustine's life would be the ones that would define him for all future ages. His life as professor had ended—his life as pastor was about to begin.

7

The Pastorate at Hippo

*W*ITH HIS POSSESSIONS SOLD, and his residence reestablished in his hometown, Augustine was ready for a quiet life of friendship and study. One day, he heard that in the nearby town of Hippo lived a member of the "agents in affairs" (a sort of "secret service" for the emperor) who wanted to speak to Augustine about how to pursue the monastic life. Immediately Augustine made the trip and encouraged the man to fulfill the vow he had made to God. Whether the man followed through on his promise, we do not know, but the trip proved important for another reason: it introduced Augustine to Valerius, the bishop of Hippo.

In fact, Augustine had on that day decided to worship with the church in Hippo. But when Bishop Valerius saw him among the crowd, he departed from his sermon, and instead spoke on the great need for clergy (presbyters[1]) in the city of Hippo. The

---

1. Unlike the office of bishop, there is some difficulty in settling on a term for this subordinate office. Often translated "priest," the word Augustine uses here is *presbyterus*. (In fact, our English word *priest* is a corruption of *presbyterus*.) The word is used throughout the New Testament to indicate one who manages or oversees a particular "flock" of the Church. It does not have the mediatorial, sacrificial aspects of "priest" in either the Old Testament or pagan Greco-Roman sense. Nevertheless, as the worship service ("mass") of the Church, and especially the Lord's Supper (Eucharist), increasingly took on sacrificial elements over the years, *presbyter* increasingly took on some of the connotations associated with Old Testament priests, making a translation decision for fourth- and fifth-century work even harder. In this work we will generally use *presbyter* to refer to Augustine's first clerical office.

35

crowd had no trouble getting the drift, and with little delay, seized Augustine and brought him to Valerius to be ordained. As we have seen with Ambrose, forcibly conscripting prominent men was not uncommon, and indeed, Augustine had purposely avoided visiting cities that were without bishops. Yet Hippo was not among these, and Augustine was only a bystander, with no thought of public ministry. The trials of life as a church officer coursed through his mind, and he protested, then wept. Misinterpreting his tears as those of ambition, the crowd now thought he wanted to be ordained bishop instead of presbyter, and assured him to just be patient! It was a rare occasion on which Augustine's skill with words failed him.

In any case, there was nothing he could do. Bishop Valerius was a shrewd man, and he was aware of the increasing threats the Church in North Africa was facing. Lingering paganism and heresies were rampant and difficult to stamp out. These included the Manichaeism that had enthralled Augustine, Arianism, and most of all, Donatism, whose adherents stressed the purity of the Church to an extreme. Such a climate demanded clergy of great ability in thought and speech, who could persuade not only the learned, but also the mass of illiterate parishioners in Hippo and beyond. Yet Valerius himself was old, and he was neither an African nor a native Latin speaker, but a Greek. Hippo needed a man who could turn a Latin phrase for the benefit of advancing the Church. Augustine, for all his reluctance, was that man.

The 37-year-old Augustine now was facing yet another upheaval in the tranquil life he had expected. Even so, he seems to have settled in quickly to his new life, accepting it as the will of God. He was allotted a house and garden by Valerius, and this he used to pursue his longstanding desire for a monastery. Here, he would live with the "servants of God," those other like-minded men of Hippo who served the Church and the community by devoted service to God. Within these walls, all was held in common, and all gifts were to be used for the advancement of Christ's Church and His kingdom.

This included Augustine's talent for study and persuasion.

Only five years ago he had left his career in rhetoric to pursue Christian retirement, yet now he found his skills as a speaker in demand once again. Contrary to longstanding African custom, Valerius now gave Augustine the responsibility of both preaching in the Church and holding public discussions and debates within the town of Hippo.

To grant such duties to a presbyter was a daring step, but also an astute one, as his colleague Possidius reveals:

> For this reason also some bishops criticized him [Valerius]. But this venerable and perceptive man, knowing this practice was customary in the eastern churches, and, taking thought for the benefit of the church, did not concern himself with the tongues of his critics, so long as his presbyter might accomplish what he himself had decided could not be, as bishop. (*Life of St. Augustine* 5)

Word of Augustine's talent spread. In 393, he had the rare privilege of addressing the General Council of Hippo, composed of Catholic bishops from across the region. For a presbyter not even 40 years old to expound the Apostles' Creed to an assembly of bishops could have bordered on impertinence, yet for Augustine it seems to have only brought him respect. Two years later, in another surprise, Valerius sought and gained approval to have Augustine appointed as co-bishop with him. A year later, Valerius died, leaving Augustine sole bishop of the city of Hippo. It would be his final office, and he held it until his death thirty-four years later.

At age 42, then, Augustine had come full circle. Raised in Thagaste, he had traveled to the center of cosmopolitanism, only to return to his hometown and then a nearby city. Set on the path of rhetoric, he had achieved the highest levels in both the academic and political worlds, only to give it all up, and then find it demanded again of him. He had left his childhood connection with the Church, embraced Manichaeism, and then found the true Christ through the medium of Cicero, Plato, and finally

Ambrose. He had left his parents to find companionship in a woman, only to have her torn from him, along with his friends, mother, and only son—and yet finally gained a band of brothers, friends, and bishops who would be his companions till his life's end. At the age of 42, when he had hoped retirement would be underway, Augustine was instead at the dawn of a new life.

8

LIFE AS BISHOP:
HERESIES, DEBATES, IMPERIAL POWER

THE BISHOP'S CHAIR THAT AUGUSTINE INHERITED IN 395 came with a heavy load. Valerius had chosen Augustine partly because he recognized in him the potential to serve the Church well in dealing with the many troubles of a bishop's life, but neither he nor his pupil Augustine could have foreseen how many there would be in the next thirty years.

An individual bishop was responsible for the physical and spiritual wellbeing of his community, to an extent that is hard to overemphasize. If members of his community suffered under physical oppression, he bore the responsibility; if they were drawn away by spiritual falsehood, it was his fault. For the rest of Augustine's life, this responsibility took center stage in everything Augustine did. The Augustine who looked forward to a retirement spent in theological contemplation and study would find himself forced to deal with matters more crucial, practical, even earthy.

Nowhere was this more pressing than in the heresies Augustine found himself facing throughout his life: Manichaeism, Arianism, Donatism, and Pelagianism. (We'll talk about the first three now and cover Pelagianism later, because of its importance to the later Church.)

Of the heresies mentioned here, Manichaeism is the hardest to define (as we have seen), and also the least persistent in Augustine's life. Indeed, while it lasted into the fourteenth century in the

Far East, its heyday in the Roman West was already coming to an end by the beginning of the fifth century. Augustine was perhaps its last famous convert there, and in converting to Catholic Christianity, he would sound the death knell for Manichaeism in Africa.

Early in his career, however, Augustine was still attempting to stamp out the traces of Manichaean sympathy in his area. In one vivid incident, Augustine (while still a presbyter) agreed to debate Fortunatus, a Manichaean figure he had known from his school days. Augustine's fellow citizens were anxious to see how their newly installed presbyter would deal with a famous Manichaean who had captivated so many from their town. Yet after barely two days of public debate, many who had been enthralled with Fortunatus no longer were. He was unable to refute even the simplest arguments of the Church, or to advance Mani's doctrine through logical reasoning. He left town soon after, never to return. Aside from public debates, Augustine continued to fight the sect on other fronts as well, devoting at least eight separate written works to the heresy. Its decline in North Africa, however, meant that his attention turned elsewhere.

Easier to define, but more troublesome for the Church, was Arianism. Its central tenet, that "there was a time when He [the Son of God] was not," was easy to understand, and compelling in its logical simplicity. It could flaunt its "literal" understanding of Scripture's teaching (in passages such as Colossians 1:15, calling Jesus the "Firstborn of all creation"), and could avoid the potential quagmires of how God the Son could be both equal with and yet in some sense dependent on the Father. For Christians who took Scripture seriously, Arianism was appealing, and so it is unsurprising that throughout the first few centuries of the Church it was a persistent foe. For some periods, it's likely that Arianism constituted the majority belief of the Church. It was the position of the converted Germanic tribes, and thus also of much of the Roman military—it even was the profession of several Roman emperors.

Thus Arianism was a hard foe to eradicate. Like all heresies, it was also a matter of public concern for Augustine, and those who taught it had to be dealt with in the open air. One such occasion

LIFE AS BISHOP: HERESIES, DEBATES, IMPERIAL POWER

occurred when Pascentius, an Arian tax official of the imperial court, had railed against the Church with charges of all sorts. Pascentius challenged Augustine to a public debate in Carthage, and Augustine accepted. From the history that remains, it appears Augustine handily won the debate. Unlike with Fortunatus, however, Pascentius did not leave in shame, but rather continued publicly protesting that he had triumphed. This went on so long that Augustine eventually addressed the situation in writing, laying out the arguments put forth at their meeting, and offering to produce witnesses to vouch for Augustine's victory. Eventually, it seems Pascentius yielded.

Other Arians struck closer to home. One of them, an Arian bishop by the name of Maximinus, came to Hippo itself teaching the Arian doctrine. With him, too, Augustine agreed to hold a public debate, but once again, afterwards Maximinus claimed to have won the debate. As with Pascentius, Augustine again wrote a document, providing details of the conference and refuting the Arian bishop.

Manichaeism and Arianism, while troublesome and empire-wide in their extent, were periodic blips on the radar of Augustine's career. Donatism, by contrast, was mostly local, deeply rooted in history, and as persistent as any heresy Augustine faced. Donatism was a theology that found its most ardent support among the poor. For these and other reasons, Augustine's handling of it was far different than his treatment of Manichaeism and Arianism, and it occupied him for some twenty years of his life.

Donatism arose as a result of the greatest persecution to have afflicted the Church. A century earlier under the emperor Diocletian, Christians across the Empire were rounded up and arrested. Clergymen could avoid this fate by betraying fellow Christians to the authorities, or by handing over their copies of the Scriptures (which, in an age before the printing press, were rare and valuable). Those clergy who complied with the imperial orders were thenceforth known by their detractors as *traditores*, a Latin word meaning both "handers over" and "traitors."

With the ascension of Constantine in 306, persecution of

Christians stopped, and with the Edict of Milan in 313, Christianity became officially tolerated throughout the Empire. Many of those who had previously denied the faith under persecution now attempted to re-enter the Church. But there were questions. Could clergy who had denied their Lord be restored to church leadership? And what about the actions they had performed in their office since betraying the Church? Were their administrations of baptism and the Lord's Supper still valid, since they had earlier betrayed their Lord and Church? The official position of the Church was that, yes, if clergy truly and publicly repented, they could be allowed back into leadership, nor was their work as ministers rendered invalid by their earlier sins.

For large swaths of the Church in Africa, however, these answers were unacceptable. The Donatists believed that even true forgiveness was not enough to wipe clean the slate of such a transgression against the Church. They also taught that the validity of a sacrament could not be separated from the condition of the man administering it. After all, if the Church was to be pure and spotless, how could it validate actions done by men who had betrayed their Lord? For the Donatists, the answer was clear, and matters soon came to a head. In 311 a suspected *traditor* consecrated a new bishop. His opponents revolted, and a rival Church was born (and led for a time by Donatus, from whom Donatism takes its name). Throughout the fourth century, then, Africa was split between two factions: Catholics and Donatists.

By the time Augustine became bishop in 396, the situation had grown increasingly desperate. The Catholic church held sway in the cities, but in the rural areas, the Donatist church was strong. Conflict in this situation was inevitable. When, for instance, a man from a Donatist church entered a Catholic one, would he be admitted to the sacraments? Would such a man need to be rebaptized if he was baptized in a Donatist church? And how should Catholic clergy and people approach interactions with their former brothers and sisters in Donatist churches?

There was violence, too. Alongside and among the Donatists were any number of groups that saw this theological dispute in

LIFE AS BISHOP: HERESIES, DEBATES, IMPERIAL POWER

very physical terms. Such groups had no hesitation about theft, assault, and even murder of opposing Catholic members. During some periods, the African countryside became awash in violence. Augustine himself at one point even faced a threat on his life.

For Augustine, the problems with the Donatists went far beyond the issues of the *traditores*. Indeed, by the time of his tenure as bishop, nearly one hundred years had passed since the persecution under Diocletian, and the *traditores* were mainly a memory. And yet the division of Africa into two rival churches had continued.

Across the world, the Church had been growing since Constantine. It had spread to the far west in Britain, to the Germanic tribes of the north, and as far east as Persia. And yet, Augustine saw in Africa a church determined to remain isolated and provincial, preening itself in its own narrow purity while the rest of the kingdom was advancing:

> *Let the whole earth tremble before His face; publish among the nations: the Lord reigns from the wood. For indeed He has made straight the earth, which shall not be moved.* What testimonies of the building of the House of God! The clouds of heaven thunder that through all the world the house of God is being built; and the frogs croak from the marsh: "We alone are Christians!" (*Expositions on the Psalms* 95.11)

Beyond this, Augustine was increasingly disquieted by the Donatists' emphasis on their own purity. As a Manichaean, he had looked up to those who could attain a level of moral purity that he could not. He had, of course, turned from this path, yet also had embraced a celibate life upon becoming a Christian. Yet, under Ambrose, he had also come to embrace a way of understanding Scripture that emphasized the spiritual meaning of its knottiest passages, which had once tripped him up. Purity was important, to be sure, but it was purity of the heart and soul that mattered most, not extreme adherence to the kind of ritual purity he saw in the Donatists' arguments.

But attaining bodily purity was a popular goal in the Christian world of his time. After Constantine, the Church (not to mention the Roman government) was increasingly filled with nominal "Christians" whose commitment extended little beyond undergoing baptism and occasionally taking the Lord's Supper. On the other hand, many Christians had reacted against such lukewarmness by renouncing this kind of life (along with their marriages, property, etc.) to pursue devoted lives with God—lives which soon made them celebrities. Augustine himself had followed this latter path, and yet Augustine soon found himself not defending such an extraordinary course, but instead the mundane, everyday life of the illiterate Christians in his flock. Despite his dramatic path to faith, Augustine had in fact become a champion of the ordinary Christian.

This came about in a variety of ways. When his friend Jerome (d. 420) wrote a pamphlet so intense in its advocacy of celibacy that it denigrated marriage, Augustine composed a work called "The Good of Marriage," intending to prevent the "greater good" of celibacy from denying the "good" of marriage that God had instituted. Or, when a prominent Roman military official asked Augustine if he should become a monk, Augustine found himself encouraging the man to *stay* in his position, arguing that the Church needed good military men. And when a woman who had taken up a vow of celibacy without her husband's agreement wrote to Augustine for advice, the bishop who himself had taken such a vow rebuked the woman for allowing the pride of her own commitments to cause her husband to stray (*Letters* 262). Across the board, Augustine defended the ordinary Christian: the Christian who sometimes ate a little bit too much, the Christian who admitted he found marital relations pleasurable as well as useful, the Christian who couldn't read Plato but who understood the words of the Gospel he heard from his bishop every Sunday. Such people were not the stuff of Christian celebrity, but in the humility of their sinful lives, they were the life of Augustine's community, and of his preaching. Such humility Augustine did not see in the Donatists.

How to *think* about the Donatists was one thing, though—how to handle them was quite another. Augustine's handling of the Donatist situation is complex. Throughout his twenty-year interaction with the situation, his methods range from persuasion to preaching to politics. Early on, as he did with the Manichaean and Arian heresies, he tried to engage leading Donatists in debate, hoping to convince them of their errors. For the most part, this didn't work. Preaching, on the other hand, seems to have been effective in preserving *his own* congregation and community against Donatist inroads. (Augustine even composed a kind of rhyming song for his mostly illiterate congregation, as a means of reminding them of the error and threat of Donatism.) Still, from what we can tell, Augustine's preaching was less successful in converting Donatists abroad.

Eventually, Augustine's approach leaned heavily on imperial authority. The Roman government since Constantine had been generally in favor of the Catholics, yet its intervention on their behalf had been hit and miss. In 395, Honorius became emperor in the West, and subsequently gave legal recognition to the Catholic Church in Africa. In the early years of the fifth century, Augustine would now leverage this legal relationship, and begin to request imperial intervention more and more. By the year 409, Honorius's government had declared that the Donatist church was heretical, and demanded that their churches be turned over to the Catholics. Thereafter, the Donatists were harshly persecuted by the imperial government, to the extent that even Augustine protested their treatment. In 412, the Donatist church was banned by imperial order.

Augustine's use of state authority to attack the Donatists is maybe the most controversial aspect of his tenure as bishop. Many have argued that his resorting to what was often a barely Christian imperial structure to crush a rival church was mere pragmatism devoid of Christian principles. Others have seen in his actions the germ of church-state collusion that would dominate the Middle Ages, for good or for ill. Still others have argued that a crusade against the Donatists unnecessarily weakened Christianity in

Africa, and led to its inability to defend against Muslim invaders years later.

Hindsight is of course 20/20. Augustine, facing the situation at the time, had to make complicated choices. Having tried persuasion for years, he became convinced that it was acceptable for the state to enter the fray. Had not God against all odds raised up Constantine to the throne? Had not God charged the civil authority in Romans 13 to advance good and punish evil? And had not God used the rod of correction throughout the Old Testament to guide His people Israel? Although not without misgivings, Augustine decided that imperial force was legitimate.

9

LIFE AS BISHOP: DAILY LIFE

*A*UGUSTINE'S FAME IN THE WESTERN WORLD rests mostly on his public reputation—his widely read works, his public actions taken in the service of the Church. For modern readers, who are often interested in the inner details of a man's life, this can be a problem, because we end up filling the gaps in what he tells us with our own preconceptions of what life must have been like before the comforts of our age. The ancients lived, we suppose, in an age of endless work, duty, and religious practice. Without modern pleasantries, life surely was a kind of drudgery for the most part. Marriages were arranged and loveless; twelve-hour workdays left no time for hobbies; vacation was unheard of; and so on. These are the thoughts that buzz about our minds. And because of these, we end up "flattening" the world of the ancients.

In some ways, Augustine is the best of ancient authors to dispel our wrong assumptions. Works like his *Confessions* and *Letters* give us an unrivaled view into the life of an ancient man. Still, Augustine is not a man of our time, and feels little need to show us every aspect of his life. Outside of *Confessions*, in fact, we learn very little from Augustine himself about his daily life.

His friends, however, tell us more. Chief among these is Possidius, a friend and fellow bishop who has left us the only ancient biography of Augustine.[1] It focuses mostly, as expected, on the

---

1. This is the *Life of St. Augustine* (*Sancti Augustini Vita*), which we quote from (as "*Life*") in the remaining chapters of this book.

major events of his life, but in the midst of this we also get a glimpse that Augustine himself never gives us.

We learn, for instance, that a principle of modesty governed the habits and possessions of Augustine and his house (recall that he lived with the other clergy of Hippo). His clothing was neither extravagant nor paltry. He mostly stayed away from rich foods and meats, but would bring out the latter for special occasions or when hospitality required it. Wine, on the other hand, was frequently present at the table, on the basis of Scripture's pronouncement that all creation was good.

More important than food for Augustine was table conduct. Gossip and unedifying speech he banished for all who ate at his table. So intense was Augustine on this point that his table bore a couplet whose sense was, "He that harms the name of an absent friend / May not as guest at this table attend" (*Life* 22). Possidius tells us that fellow clergy who didn't heed this rule faced a strong warning from Augustine. No less serious than idle talk were oaths. Augustine forbade his clergy from making them, on the grounds that it was best to steer far away from being condemned as an oath breaker. And if anyone forgot this rule and uttered an oath, there was a consequence: he lost one drink. Before a meal, it was preset how many drinks each man could have, and he could lose some of these by misconduct. Violations of table rules were punished where it really mattered!

Even stricter than these were Augustine's self-imposed regulations on contact with women. In the house where he and the clergy lived, no woman was allowed to stay. The reason was, in part, for purity's sake, but also had much to do with the testimony of the church to the outside world. Even the appearance of evil (1 Thess. 5:22) was to be avoided, lest a stumbling block be put in the way of others. Indeed, Possidius tells us that even Augustine's own sister and nieces (who had undertaken a life of celibacy) came under this rule, and never stayed with Augustine in the house. Women could, of course, meet and speak with him on a variety of topics, but only with another member of the clergy present—never alone.

LIFE AS BISHOP: DAILY LIFE

A bishop's life was one of endless counsel, adjudication, and confrontation. Over the 350 years of the Church's existence, the bishop had come to occupy an increasingly greater place in the lives of his parishioners. As the Roman Empire weakened and gradually disintegrated in the centuries following, it was to the bishop that men would look for advice, judgments, and protection. Such questions were time consuming, with spiritual implications:

> Consequently, when he was appealed to either by Christians or by any group of men, he would hear their causes attentively and dutifully.... Even for those which sometimes occupied him all the way until dinner (other times, however, he would fast the entire day), he nonetheless would always examine the cases, and, glimpsing in them the condition of Christian souls, would analyze how much each man was either progressing in faith and good works, or declining from these. And when he found opportunity, he taught both parties the truth of the divine Law, and impressed it upon them; and both taught and admonished them how eternal life might be gained: asking nothing else from those with whom he spent this time except Christian obedience and commitment, which is owed to both God and men, reproving sinners before all, so the rest might have fear: and he did this as one ordained by the Lord as a watchman over the house of Israel, preaching the word and insisting in season, out of season, reproving, exhorting, rebuking with all longsuffering and instruction; and he gave special attention to instruct those who were able to teach others also. (*Life* 19)

And so, even in Augustine's time, people pressed him on any number of topics, from disputes over inheritances, to questions of land ownership, to educational advice. One man asked him to write a eulogy for his dead wife—Augustine ended up declining (we'll see why later). One wannabe poet asked Augustine to evaluate his attempt at Virgilian epic poetry—Augustine asked why he was bothering him with foolish matters. Another friend even asked him for advice on stopping the slave trade—despite

Augustine's and the clergy's efforts, the Christian empire was still involved in the mire of slavery.

One other exchange of correspondence[2] will illustrate the situations Augustine faced. In 419–420, Augustine learned that a nun in an estate outside his hometown had been raped. The guilty man was apparently the supervisor of the estate, which was owned by a Catholic landowner named Dorotheus. When the crime was discovered, the rapist had been excommunicated. In learning of the crime, Augustine did two things. First, he wrote to the clergy of Thagaste (including his friend Alypius), informing them of his judgment that the man should be further punished by being removed as estate supervisor. But second, he wrote the landowner Dorotheus, informing him that further punishment was necessary, but that it ought not be overly severe. Augustine, who was not opposed to capital punishment, nonetheless had to walk a careful line. The situation involved theological concerns (excommunication), judicial elements (punishment of the rape), and practical, monetary issues (the well-being of Dorotheus's estate), and so Augustine tried to ensure that the crime would be justly punished but with mercy, so that Dorotheus would become a scandal neither to the church nor to the world. Such situations were par for the course for Augustine's everyday life.

---

2. For more, see *Letters* 14*.

10

Life as Bishop: Writing and Preaching

*F*rom the first days of his education, until his death, Augustine's life was dominated by writing: "I aim to be one of those who write in order to make progress, and who make progress by writing" (*Letters* 143.2)." As a bishop, Augustine had to address topics far outside the typical ones that occupied a professor of rhetoric. Before, Augustine wrote for philosophers and rhetoricians; now, his audience included both the rich and famous as well as the poor and lowly, and his subject matter embraced all aspects of their lives, from birth to death.

But more than anything, Augustine's way of writing and speaking now was molded by Scripture. Indeed, it is impossible to exaggerate how deeply Augustine imbibed Scripture. One scholar (Henri Marrou) has estimated he quotes from it over forty-two thousand times in his writings! Across his mature works, barely a sentence goes by without a reference, quotation, or allusion to some part of Scripture. For us, such a practice seems impossible, tethered as we are to the physical (or electronic) copies of Scripture we possess. But we must remember that the ancient world was a world of speech and a world of memory, where books were rare and memories well exercised. For a man of Augustine's training, who memorized in school the entire Roman epic the *Aeneid*, memorizing Scripture was natural (and expected):

His memory, trained on classical texts, was phenomenally active. In one sermon, he could move through the whole Bible, from Paul to Genesis and back again, via the Psalms, piling half-verse on half-verse. This method of exegesis indeed, which involved creating a whole structure of verbal echoes, linking every part of the Bible, was particularly well-suited to teaching this hitherto quite unknown text, to an audience used to memorizing by ear.[1]

There survive some five million words of Augustine's writing, far more than of any other ancient author. It has even been calculated that Augustine wrote the equivalent of a three-hundred-page book each year from the age of 40 until his death at age 76. When we recall that all this writing was done either by his own hand or by that of his stenographers (by dictation), the feat is a stunning one indeed. (Augustine kept copies of most of his works in his own library, but admits in his memoriam *Reconsiderations* that some of his books have been lost over the years, some because of delinquent borrowers!)

What works make up this vast output? The genre of writing is exceptionally broad, from autobiography to anti-heretical works, from apologetic writings defending the Christian faith to scriptural expositions and commentaries, and from theological and moral works to practical advice on daily living. Augustine wrote treatises on subjects such as education, marriage, burial, lying, preaching, and finding happiness in life. We give here only a few highlights; a more complete listing can be found in the appendix.

Along with *Confessions*, Augustine's letter output gives the clearest, most comprehensive view of his life. The letters cover his entire Christian lifetime, from 386 to his death in 430. They engage people from every part of his life, from personal friends, to parishioners, to political and imperial figures, to church authorities, to fellow bishops, to Christian celebrities, and more. One letter is written in response to a single woman who had asked Augustine how to pray. Another is to the famous bishop Cyril of

---

[1]. Peter Brown, *Augustine of Hippo: A Biography* (University of California Press, 2000), 251.

LIFE AS BISHOP: WRITING AND PREACHING

Alexandria, explaining and asking for help against the Pelagian heresy. Many letters address his longtime friends, Nebridius, Alypius, and Paulinus of Nola, on matters both official and personal. There's even a letter to the monastery where Augustine's sister presided, imposing some new (and apparently necessary) guidelines for the nuns to follow.

Last but not least, there is Augustine's large output of sermons. Comprising over four hundred (some are still being discovered—the most recent in 2007), they extend the length of Augustine's preaching career, and show how the bishop of Hippo addressed his congregation on Sundays throughout the year, as well as on special occasions, like Easter and feast days.

In many ways, his sermons show us a very different Augustine than the one we find in *Confessions* and *City of God*. Reading those works, one might imagine Augustine only in his elaborate, high-style form, but in his sermons, we see how Augustine had to change the style he knew in order to reach a congregation that was illiterate and fonder of popular culture than classical training. And so, instead of long, complex sentences, in Augustine's sermons we find short, pithy statements full of rhyme, repetition, and even puns. Augustine has a plan for his words, of course, but he also improvises, jokes around, and gestures—all to ensure that his flock understands and retains the point he is making.

To read Augustine's sermons is also to realize that he was pastor to a particular flock. Particular flocks have particular problems, and so each sermon is delivered with all the intimacy and directness that came from facing the people every week whose sins he knew well. In the wake of barbarian attack, for example, Augustine exhorts his flock not to forget caring for the poor. Or, in his farewell sermon to his congregation, we see him asking them to care for his successor as they have for him. And very often, we see him interacting with his congregation, interrupting his sermon with exclamations as he reacts to the words (and likely, facial expressions) of his congregation.

Augustine the rhetorician had thus become Augustine the pastor. His sermons reveal that his aspirations toward Rome and

Milan had now been left far behind. These were now replaced by work with people who knew little of the orators Cicero and Demosthenes, but rather of the fishermen James and John, and of their Lord. As Augustine preached each week, his old rhetorical models were gradually supplanted.

And yet, as Augustine moved into his forties, it soon became clear that even while the Empire of Rome gave way to the kingdom of Christ, old enemies were again making their presence known. Rome, secure for hundreds of years, was now in Christian times being attacked by barbarians thought to have been vanquished. It was yet another surprise for Augustine: for the final twenty years of his life, the world he had put away and taken for granted would now threaten the Church he had embraced. In the year 410, Augustine the Christian would need to become Augustine the Roman once again.

11

The Sack of Rome

On August 24, 410, a Germanic tribe under the command of a mercenary Gothic general named Alaric sacked the city of Rome. It was the first time in nearly eight hundred years that the city had seen such an invasion. Even as the borders of the Empire gradually contracted under pressure from external tribes, the city of Rome itself had long retained its aura as eternal and impregnable. But now, the citizens of Rome faced the prospect of hostile tribes invading at will. Augustine's fellow churchman Jerome summed up the shock that many felt: "The city that seized the whole world was itself seized."[1]

The backstory to the sack of Rome is long and complex, and subject to considerable disagreement among historians.[2] Suffice it to say that at least a century of misfortunes and bad policies by Roman emperors and officials took its toll in 410 on Rome and its citizens.

For three days, Gothic forces stripped, burned, and pillaged the city. Buildings were destroyed, houses were invaded and looted. Some residents were taken captive; others were beaten, raped, or killed. By the standards of the time the loss of life was small, but the attack rippled through the Empire. In Bethlehem, Jerome reacted in shock and grief:

---

1. Jerome, *Letters* 127.12.
2. Much of the controversy focuses on how abrupt, violent, and sudden were the "barbarian invasions" of the 400s.

> Who would believe that the Rome which was built up by conquering the whole world could collapse? That she who was mother of all nations should become also their tomb? ... That every day in this holy Bethlehem we would be taking in noblemen and noblewomen who were once abounding in all riches, but now are beggars? (*Commentary on Ezekiel*, preface to book 3)

For those of us living in the West in the twenty-first century, such reactions may strike us as over the top. Not since World War II has western Europe seen such an invasion, and the United States never has. We can try to capture something of the tenor of the year 410 by imagining one of our capitals attacked: Washington, or London, or Paris. Indeed, we might remember the terrorist attacks that all three capitals have experienced in the last twenty years. Those who can recall the fear and raw emotion of September 11, 2001, may have some grid to understand the events of AD 410.

Yet even this comparison falls short of the immensity of this event to Roman citizens. For us, Washington is not the United States, nor London the United Kingdom; but for Romans, in a very real way, Rome *was* the Empire. All of the national mythology hearkened back to that city on the Tiber river, founded over one thousand years previous. All of their historical heroes had left their mark on that city. And such was the splendor of Rome that it had affected virtually every area of a citizen's experience, from his taxes, to his military service, to his "Roman" alphabet (which we still use today). Rome was the incarnation of power, riches, wealth, culture, religion, and history—everything that made a Roman a Roman. But in 410, all of that was now up for grabs.

We can easily see why old-school, pagan Romans reacted with horror to the sack of their city, but what about Christians? After all, Rome was where the apostles Peter and Paul had given their lives as martyrs. Rome was the longtime persecutor of the faith, and was seen by many as a stronghold of sinful decadence. Would not Christians see in the sack of Rome, if not a triumph, then at least a vindication of their faith?

On the contrary, most of the reactions that survive from Christians of this period are not of this sort. Christianity had been legal for a century, and perhaps this period of calm had eroded some of the Christian hostility toward Rome as persecutor. Indeed, instead of satisfaction at the downfall of Rome, what we find among Christians is shock that a city so long established could ever fall, and fear about what that portended. As Jerome put it, "What is safe, if Rome perishes?"[3] Among Christians we also find great uncertainty about what the political future of their world would be. And we find a growing tendency toward insularity—a batten-down-the-hatches mentality that might allow them to survive the onslaught, but was little help in promoting Christian service and outreach.

All of these reactions and more we see in Augustine and his flock at Hippo. His first reactions are muted. In a couple of sermons, he alludes to the event by reminding his congregation that adversity is part of the life of a Christian, and that the life to come should be the Christian's true focus. Turning his congregation's attention to the crumbling amphitheater in Hippo, he asks them to consider that the extravagance of its godless builders was now giving way to decay.

As time goes on, however, Augustine becomes more direct in his reference to the crisis. In one sermon, we see that evidently his congregation's shock had turned to fear about the future. They had thought Rome was indestructible; now, what did its downfall mean for them? Augustine sympathizes with their astonishment, but sees the events as perfectly in line with a world that has grown old:

> Are you surprised that the world is falling apart? Well, be surprised then that the world has grown old. It's like a man: he's born, grows, gets old. . . . The world has grown old; it's full of burdens. Has God provided too little for you because he sent you Christ in the world's old age? . . . Of course, the world had to be full of

3. Jerome, *Letters* 123.17

troubles: He came to both comfort you amidst those troubles, and to assure you of rest for eternity. Don't eagerly hang on to an old world, and be unwilling to grow young in Christ, who tells you, "The world is perishing, the world is aging, the world is falling apart; it labors with the gasps of old age. Don't fear, *your youth shall be made new like the eagle's*." (*Sermons* 81.8)

Augustine's reaction to his congregation reflects the pastoral skill he's gained. This is not the Augustine who had hoped to retire in Christian contemplation, but instead the Augustine of nearly twenty years of pastoral work. He engages, to be sure, the intellectual question of what the sack of Rome represents, but he also engages the hearts and fears of his flock. Unlike Jerome, Augustine's pastoral experience had distanced him somewhat from classical culture, and so he had seen that the kingdom of God could and would endure outside the hallowed walls of Rome. In one of his tenderest disclosures, we get a glimpse of how Augustine himself perceives the possible end of his own civilization:

"Look," [someone] says, "in Christian times Rome has perished." Perhaps Rome has not perished: perhaps it's been scourged, not executed: perhaps it's been punished, not destroyed. Perhaps Rome is not perishing if Romans aren't perishing. In other words, they won't perish, if they praise God: perish they will if they blaspheme Him. For what is Rome if not the Romans? . . . [The whole city] was made in such a way that someday it would fall to ruin. . . . *Heaven and earth will pass away*; what's so surprising, then, if someday a city meets its end? And perhaps the city's end is not just yet; still, someday or other it will be the city's end. (*Sermons* 81.9)

Augustine's response here shows both the humanity and maturity of his thought. He defers on the question of whether this sack of Rome is a final punishment for its sins. Rome may last, or it may fall—who can tell? We hear in such a statement a remarkable coincidence of the elements of Augustine's life. He had been, from birth, a Roman, of course, and he clearly retains here a hope that Rome is *not* finally destroyed. Yet we also see that his final hope lies not in Rome, but in the kingdom of God—and it is this that Augustine holds out before his congregation. Rome was, in the end, but a human creation, and as such, it was no remarkable thing to say that it would end. Indeed, Augustine had seen his own plans dashed throughout his life, and had seen what glories God had wrought in accordance with His will. Instead of fearing the future, then, his intent is to fix his congregation's gaze upon the eternal kingdom, "where neither moth nor rust doth corrupt" (Matt. 6:20). If the destruction of the Empire was God's will for His people, they could trust that. And they could trust that the kingdom of Rome was vastly outdone by the kingdom that would never perish.

But in Augustine's final sermons on the sack of Rome, we see him concerned with another line of attack on his flock: specifically, that Christianity was harmful for a nation and its citizens. After all, if Rome prospered until it embraced Christianity, was it not Christianity that was to blame for the attack?

In 410, a sizable minority of the Empire's population was still not Christian, and many of those who claimed Christianity were nominal at best in their commitment. In the months following the sack of Rome, Christianity increasingly came to bear the brunt of the blame in respected intellectual circles. Christians, such as Augustine, who had come to see their faith triumph at the official level, now faced the prospect of men in high circles doubting its usefulness to the Empire. If Christ couldn't protect the Empire from a band of roving Germans, what use was there in Rome following Him?

For Augustine, this was a question that needed answering, and answering in full. Doing so would take him some fifteen years, and cause him to revisit not only the history of the world, but of his own life. Augustine had grown up Roman, lived in Rome, and worked in Rome, only to reject that life and return to Africa. His work with his flock had been decidedly un-Roman in its qualities, even as he shared their grief at the sack of their city. Now, however, the attack on Christian faith was coming at a new level, from the finest intellects of the day. To defeat this attack, he would need to marshal all the past learning he had long ago put away. He would now need to beat the rhetoricians at their own game, and his massive attempt at doing so would become his magnum opus, *The City of God.*

12

City of God

The sack of Rome was in many ways a wake-up call. Augustine himself would later note that it could have been much worse. There was, after all, little loss of life in the sack itself, and the Arians, though heretics, drew back from slaying Catholics who fled into the church buildings. Yet the sack exploded any illusion that Rome was impregnable, or that the security of the world they knew could be taken for granted.

Across the Empire, and especially in the intellectual centers of the great cities, the sack also set in motion a discussion that would consume the next fifteen years of Augustine's life. Though much of the Empire had become Christianized, many of the old Roman families remained resolutely pagan. Dispersed by the turmoil at Rome, they now found their way as refugees to cities such as Carthage, where the buzz became all about whether Christianity was "useful" in light of the recent crisis.

Among these young aristocrats was a 30-year-old named Volusianus. He was a bright young man of ancient Roman stock, with a mother and niece who were famous Christians with connections to Augustine. Yet Volusianus himself remained doubtful of Christian teaching, with objections on matters ranging from the virgin birth to the humanity of Christ. Most of all, he was unconvinced that Christianity provided a proper basis on which to govern the Roman state. After the sack of Rome, it was an open question whether a Christian empire was not a contradiction in terms.

Prodded by Volusianus's mother, Augustine wrote to him, beginning a series of letters between the two men, joined eventually by the imperial (and dependably Christian) official Marcellinus, who had helped Augustine oppose the Donatists. The conversation continued for a year or so, but Augustine's explanations seemed unable to convince Volusianus. He and his generation held allegiance not to the Church, but rather to the ancient philosophical ideas of the Roman world.

Thirty years previous, Augustine himself had sailed the streams of this refined philosophical tradition. As chair of rhetoric at Milan, he had taught men like Volusianus, and the present danger posed by a movement of intellectuals was not lost on him. Twenty years previous, he had given up that life to begin a very different one caring for the citizens of Hippo. But that was in a more assured time, when a man could have confidence that Christianity as a political power would continue. The Christian (and Catholic) Theodosius was ruler of all the Empire, and much of the world seemed safe for the average citizen. But in the intervening years, uncertainty had emerged. Theodosius was dead, governance of the Empire was split between East and West, and Rome had been sacked by the barbarians. Such an environment seemed hostile to the spread of Christianity, and there was potential for men like Volusianus to channel and harden this opposition to Christianity.

Even so, Augustine hesitated at first to engage this conflict. He seems to have hoped that his earlier, informal letters would allay the objections coming from intellectual circles. Yet Marcellinus soon asked for more: not simply a series of letters, but a larger work, a "full, illuminating, and magnificent reply" to the arguments that filled the air in Carthage (*Letters* 136.3).

A year or so later, in 413, the first installment of Augustine's response appeared—three books of what would become the twenty-two-book tome *City of God*. It would not be completed until at least 425 (perhaps even 429), and would constitute by far the longest, most involved, and most laborious work of

Augustine's career. Its first part comprises five books addressing those who trusted in paganism for their happiness and security in this world, and five books critiquing those who looked to philosophy for their future. Its second, larger part covers in twelve additional books the identity, origin, progress, and future of all mankind, divided into two "cities," one of God, and the other of man. With such scope comes exhaustive scrutiny, even by Augustine's own standards. No matter seems beyond inquiry, whether it's the nature of free will, the psychology of assault, the origin of evil, or whether pygmies truly exist! Indeed, so massive is the scale of this work (Augustine himself calls it a *magnum opus*) that few have read it in full, and it tends to be known more in excerpt.

In *City of God*, readers encounter an Augustine whose writing style is different than that of *Confessions*, *Sermons*, or *Letters*. In responding to the accusations of intellectuals, Augustine reaches back to a style he had abandoned when he became a Christian: that of late Roman intellectual discourse. It is a strategy calculated to show that he knew the world of Roman high-style intellectuals and could beat them at their own game. And so Augustine references and quotes constantly from all the bright lights of Latin literature and philosophy—Sallust, Cicero, Livy, Virgil—bringing their words into sharp relief with the words of Scripture to show the latter's superiority. It is an approach designed in word, sound, and argument to obliterate any reliance on the ancient system of paganism, and to issue a complete, final, and comprehensive rejection of that paganism as a basis for Roman law, government, or culture.

To accomplish this, Augustine attacks the assumptions of his opponents: for one, that in past times, following ancient paganism resulted in good fortune for the Roman state. He challenges this notion by showing that ills happen to both good and bad men alike, and are not necessarily tied to the conduct they maintain. Moreover, the Romans themselves experienced terrible calamities while giving dutiful worship to the gods, evidenced most directly by the fall and burning of Troy (the mythical progenitors of the Romans). If such happened to the Romans under paganism, how can they then accuse Christianity of being responsible for a sack much smaller in scale?

Such a tactic shows Augustine had lost none of the shrewd logic of his younger years. Yet he also shows a desire to turn the argument toward spiritual matters by revealing the conceit in the Roman definition of "calamity." The Romans may have longed for the days of material, economic, or imperial prosperity, but such consideration ignored the *spiritual* calamities they were experiencing. They could not justly condemn adultery, for the very gods they worshiped were adulterous. They could not extol peace, for the gods they worshiped were contentious and quarrelsome, as were the later political leaders of Rome. Over and over, the Romans showed that their embrace of paganism brought them calamities of the soul far greater than those of the body.

One sin in particular becomes the focus of Augustine's attack: the lust for rule (*libido dominandi*). Here, Augustine takes a phrase from the classical historian Sallust, but expands its meaning. Sallust had commented with sadness that man no longer desired good behavior, because of a greed for dominating others. Augustine goes even further, arguing that Rome's love of glory is really a cover for a love of power and domination. Augustine's argument here is larger than life, and yet also completely characteristic. We have seen in *Confessions* and elsewhere how Augustine blames external evil on sins of the heart. "Out of the overflow of the heart, the mouth speaks" (Matt. 12:34). Or in this case, out of the lust of its own citizens' hearts came Rome's love of power and domination.

This central theme shapes much of *City of God*. In the second half of the work, this sin becomes one of the many features that distinguish the City of Man from the City of God. From its inception in the Fall of Adam, the City of Man seeks to love, possess, and dominate what it does not have, and has no satisfaction in what it does have. The sins of envy, pride, greed, and lust characterize it down through the ages, until its final destruction at the last judgment.

Indeed, it was impossible not to consider sin and judgment

when trying to explain the traumatic events of 410. But here, Augustine is surprisingly circumspect. Some of his contemporaries had thundered in high dudgeon that the troubles of Rome were punishment for its sins. But Augustine draws back from this conclusion, declining to assert a direct link between the sack and specific sins of the Romans. For him, the sack of Rome, whatever lessons it might teach, was an event whose meaning could only be fully understood in eternity.

Nor did Augustine stand outside of the crisis as a delighted spectator. As we have seen, he was an unabashed Roman (as was the Apostle Paul), and he was not averse to praising Rome's virtues when praise was due. He was willing to grant that, as bad as Rome was, it was perhaps still better than those empires before it.[1] Honor, glory, loyalty—these were ideals that *did* characterize the Romans of old, Augustine could admit. And for that, he was willing to praise them—while reminding his reader that even the good virtues of pagans come from the providence of God.

And here is one of Augustine's most influential ideas. As anxious as he is to distinguish the City of Man and the City of God, Augustine nonetheless emphasizes that, in this world, the two cities are mingled together inseparably on their distinctive journeys.

Because of this, the City of God could legitimately use the morsels of truth it found in Roman or pagan literature, so long as it used them toward an advancement of its own spiritual goals. And while it sojourned together with the City of Man, it could and must contribute to the well-being of that city, as far as it was able.

This is a crucial element of Augustine's philosophy. In his time, the separation between Church and world had begun to erode. Where being a Christian had once meant persecution, now it might mean advancement. And as increasing numbers of illustrious pagans claimed Christian faith, the reality of what defined a true Christian was becoming murky.

On the other hand, Christianity had now spread to outlying corners of the world (Britain, and even Ireland). Closer to

---

1. See, e.g., *City of God* 2.21, 2.29; *Letters* 138.3.16–17.

home, Christianity had begun to splinter into various sects as opinions on doctrine began to diverge. In such an environment, the comingling of the cities of God and of man helped explain reality. Within the physical boundaries of the City of Man lived many who were true citizens of the City of God. Correspondingly, within the *visible* City of God resided many who were *not* its true citizens. "Many sheep without—many wolves within"—this would come to define Augustine's conception of the Church. While these cities sojourned on earth, they existed comingled, but there would come a day when God's judgment would make the boundaries clear.

Indeed, more than any other of Augustine's works, *City of God* points toward the future. In a world shaken by the events of 410, men looked for a place to find stability. The intellectuals whom Augustine addressed in *City of God* looked for stability in the literature and traditions of the past—in the "eternal city" of Rome. By contrast, Augustine points his audience to something truly permanent: the City of God. As Peter Brown puts it, "Augustine drains the glory from the Roman past in order to project it far beyond the reach of men, into the 'Most glorious City of God.'"[2] By demolishing Roman claims to virtue and glory, he can present his readers that glory in its true form, in Christ—to be fully realized only in heaven.

As Augustine comes to the conclusion of this immense work, these are the thoughts that fire his mind. How will redeemed bodies exist in heaven? Will they be unclothed, and if so, how will there be no sexual lust? Will infants who perished be resurrected as infants, or as adults?

Such considerations lead Augustine to a remarkable series of observations, as he contemplates the terrible pains and tragedies of life. It is a section of sensitivity and perception, and it reveals Augustine's years of work as a pastor. The man who taught rhetoric at Rome could never have felt these pains so acutely, but the man who had seen them afflict his congregation was well able to do so:

---

2. Brown, *Augustine of Hippo*, 311.

Who walks anywhere without being subject to unexpected accidents? Some old man with feet in good shape fell on his way home from the forum, broke his foot, and died from this wound. What seems safer than sitting down? Yet Eli the priest fell from the chair he was sitting in and died. Farmers—no, actually, all of us—how many and how great are the disasters we fear to our crops, from heaven and earth and destructive animals! ... Then too, as regards the body itself there are so many evils of disease that not even the doctors' books can contain them all; in most, maybe all of them, even the cures and treatments themselves are torments.... Has not hunger brought [men] to such a point that they cannot even keep themselves from the flesh of men, and so consume them—and not men they find already dead, but those they have slain for that purpose? And to such a point that mothers consume not some stranger or other, but even their own sons, with an unbelievable savagery caused by fierce hunger! And finally, there is sleep itself, which rightly bears the name of "rest"—but who can explain in words how often it actually becomes "unrest" from the visions of its dreams, and how it wretchedly disturbs our soul and senses with so many terrors (even if of things not real), which it holds out and represents to us in such a way that we cannot distinguish them from what is real? (*City of God* 22.22)

Augustine's answer to these questions is simple: "From this hellish existence of our miserable lives nothing delivers us but the grace of Christ." And, characteristically, Augustine's purpose for the list of pains is not to give incentive for complaint, but rather occasion for praise in contemplating all the blessings that fill the world. Even in its fallen state, the world was unimaginably beautiful by the decree of its Creator:

Now as for the rest of creation, what language would be enough to tell of its beauty and usefulness which the divine bounty has granted man to wonder at and to use? ... Shall we speak of the manifold and varied beauty of the sky and earth and sea; of the sheer wealth and wondrous appearance of light itself; of the sun and moon and stars; of the shady dark of the woods; of the colors and fragrances of flowers; of the variety and multitude of chattering and painted birds; of the diverse kinds of so many and such splendid animals, the smallest of which hold more wonder for us (for we are more astonished by the works of ants and bees than by the vast bodies of whales)? Or how about also the sheer grandeur of the sea itself, when it decks itself with varied colors as if with garments, and is sometimes green (and this in many shades), at other times purple, still other times blue? (*City of God* 22.24)

Shortly after, after thousands of lines written in twenty-two books over the course of fifteen years, Augustine closes his work with the simple remark "I am done," along with one final reference to the debt he paid by writing this work. The instigator of that debt, Marcellinus, had been long dead by the time Augustine finished the work, but in truth, Augustine did far more than was requested of him. Defending Christianity against intellectual attacks was the presenting issue, but in the end it allowed him to work out themes he had meditated on for years. Objections against Christianity had begun the work, but praise of God's endless providential blessings would now bring it to an end:

> Who could ever bring everything to mind? Indeed these items alone, which I have pressed together as into a bundle, if I should wish to untie what I've tied together and unwrap it, what delay there would be in dealing with each item contained there! And all these are but consolations for the wretched and damned, not rewards for the blessed. What therefore shall be the rewards, if the consolations are so many and of such a sort and so great? What shall He give those He predestined to life, who has given all these things even to those He predestined to death? (*City of God* 22.24)

13

Pelagianism

The most famous, lengthy, and vicious controversy Augustine ever faced was begun not by *City of God* or any of his more ambitious theological works, but by his *Confessions*. In the early 400s, this work from ten years previous ignited a storm that would occupy Augustine the rest of his life, and consume his entire last decade in writing and arguing.

The trigger for this was a simple, almost off-the-cuff statement from book 10 of *Confessions*, reflecting Augustine's difficulty in obeying God's commands: "Grant what You command, and command what You will" (10.29.40).

At a public recitation of *Confessions,* a certain man heard this line, and rose up in anger, amazed that anyone would need to ask God for the ability to do what He had already commanded.

That man was Pelagius, a name that would be infamously linked with Augustine forever after. Yet to understand the nature of the conflict that would develop, it is helpful to have a sense of the world in which Pelagius lived. By the fifth century, persecution of Christians had ceased for nearly a century. At that time almost no one lived who had experienced the painful, yet also purifying, oppression of persecution. Under Constantine, the Church had gained not only a protector but also a benefactor, and as favor from Rome increased, so did the visible, physical presence of the Church. Church buildings grew in both size and splendor.

Catholic doctrine (as we've seen in the Donatist controversy) increasingly found a friend in many of the emperors.

As Christianity became less a stigma and more a sign of the future, the Church's membership swelled with increasing numbers of those who saw the handwriting on the wall. One consequence of this was that a great many of those within the visible Church bore little resemblance in their faith to those poor, harassed Christians of yesteryear. It was now politically useful to be a Christian.

Christians of the time were aware of this problem, and it resulted in a movement towards reform and, increasingly, monasticism. When being Christian meant little more than a bare profession, perhaps the true mark of a Christian was withdrawal, and dedication to ascetic piety, rigor, and good works. This was the conclusion reached by a growing number of reformers.

Pelagius was one of these. He came from the furthest reaches of the Empire, in Britain, but had achieved some fame as an ethical reformer dedicated to practical (and ascetic) Christianity. His concern with Augustine's plea for grace, then, was not so much its impact on theology, but rather its effect on practical Christian living. If a man believed he had no capability within him to do good, would he not give up and turn to sin?

This was the question. It was not that Pelagius was unconcerned with sin—rather the reverse. He had no trouble believing in the *reality* of sin—his concern was what that sin *represented*. What exactly was it that kept man from doing good? Was it, as Augustine seemed to imply, a deep, abiding corruption in a man? Or was it simply the burden of habit—an accumulation of sinful choices? If Augustine's famous prayer—"Grant what You command, and command what You will"—were correct, would not that mean God was commanding what was impossible, or violating human freedom?

This question of whether man had freedom to do good was the central dilemma. Specifically, what exactly was meant by *freedom*? Pelagius conceived of freedom as the possibility and condition of right action, so that if a man possessed "natural freedom," knew of God's law and Word, made good choices, and so on, he had the ability to act rightly in his nature. That men did *not* act rightly reflected nothing about their nature, but only their choices and habit (though Pelagius did affirm it was possible to be sinless). This meant Pelagius was adamant on the one hand about man's ability to do good, and on the other hand about the justice of God's punishment if he was not. There were "the righteous" and the "condemned," and no middle ground. Men who were condemned had no recourse to mercy, because they had failed to use their free will to do good.

Augustine, too, held to freedom of the will, but in a different way. Adam had the ability to sin or not to sin, it was true, but Adam lost that full freedom by an improper, sinful use of the will. From then on, he and his descendants operated under a will whose freedom consisted only in vain choices. True liberty of the will was only restored upon conversion, which allowed the will again to function properly. Christians, therefore, lived in a transitory state, able to exercise true freedom by choosing good, yet also retaining the root of corruption from Adam within them. Their final glory would occur after death, when at long last they would possess the inability to sin, and the root of sin finally would be removed.

These ideas were at the center of the disagreement, but other questions swirled around. How exactly was Adam's sin passed on to his posterity, and what was the nature of the effect? Was death the chief consequence of the Fall, or was there also an abiding guilt that accompanied it? And how was an "inclination to sin" to be understood? For a man such as Pelagius, "death passing upon all men" was simply a way of speaking of the force of sinful habit that Adam instituted, which then implicated men because of their incorrect use of their free will. For Augustine, original sin was much deeper, a root of corruption that indwelt all men from conception.

Given such stark contrasts, it is perhaps surprising that Augustine did not immediately enter the fray when he heard of Pelagius's objections. Yet He had never met Pelagius, and it seems that his knowledge of Pelagius's actual views was uncertain. It may also be that Augustine was sympathetic to Pelagius's concern for practical righteousness. After all, as a Manichaean, Augustine had known what it was to blame one's nature for his sins, and to claim that the burden of sin fell not on himself, but on an alien nature he could not control. Augustine, too, probably saw the growing lack of practical holiness, in both his own flock and in the Church and imperial government abroad. And so for a time, Augustine watched from a distance.

In the years after 410, however, this changed. The sack of Rome dispersed many Roman Christians abroad, and among these were not only Pelagius, but a disciple of his named Caelestius. As often happens, the younger man held positions more extreme than those of his master, claiming that Adam would have died even had he not sinned, that death was therefore *not* a punishment, and that infants were born as pure as Adam was.

This last item brought the controversy home to something very physical: infant baptism. The practice had long been widespread in the Church, and then, as now, Christians baptized infants for a variety of reasons (some drawn more from Scripture, others less so). But Caelestius's teaching focused the argument: for even if the doctrinal details about baptism remained unsettled, it was clear that to deny *any* need for baptism was to attack the doctrine and culture of the historic Church. With baptism, the debate now became not academic, but tangible.

And this brought Augustine's first salvos in the developing war, not against Pelagius specifically, but his disciple Caelestius. Against the younger man's teachings, Augustine maintained that infants *do* need baptism because they inherit Adam's corruption, and so stand condemned without being born again of water and the Spirit.[1] This was only the tip of the iceberg for Augustine, though. As the conflict continued, and as Augustine obtained authentic works of Pelagius, he broadened his focus, and began to oppose Pelagius and Caelestius more directly by the year 415.

---

1. As was common in the Church of his day, Augustine accepted the doctrine of baptismal regeneration: that the waters of baptism caused the recipient to be born again of the Spirit. On this, the magisterial reformer John Calvin and many subsequent reformers found fault with Augustine's teaching.

That same year, the controversy might have ended in Jerusalem, where Pelagius was brought up on heresy charges. Yet sympathy for Pelagius carried the day for a time. Later that year, Pelagius again avoided defeat by publicly issuing corrections of misunderstandings that had arisen, and more important, by repudiating some of the more extreme teachings of Caelestius. To all appearances, the Christian East was prepared to vindicate Pelagius, and even in the West, objection was not uniform.

Yet in Africa, opposition was strong, and a council condemned Pelagianism in 416. But Rome was not Africa, and when the African bishops sent their decision to Innocent, the bishop of Rome, he approved only a watered-down version of the Africans' condemnation. Matters worsened when, upon Innocent's death, Pelagius and Caelestius appealed his decision to the new bishop of Rome, Zosimus, who promptly declared their views unobjectionable. Not to be dissuaded, the Africans continued to hold councils, issue judgments that supported the doctrine of original sin, and attack Pelagianism.

The controversy went on. Finally, in 418, the imperial Roman court weighed in on the side of Augustine and the African Church. Pelagius and Caelestius were condemned as heretics by the court, and soon after by the bishop of Rome, who acquiesced to the court's ruling. Bishops who resisted the imperial order were to be excommunicated, and Pelagius and Caelestius fled to the East, where they took refuge with sympathetic bishops. Officially, the controversy was now closed, but in fact the battle lingered. Pelagius and Caelestius faded quickly from the scene of history, but they had made their mark on those who supported their ideas.

One such man was Julian, bishop of Eclanum. Though he was only one of those excommunicated for refusing to abide by the court's decision, he was also uniquely loud in his criticisms of Augustine. In Augustine's doctrine Julian saw nothing less than Manichaeism reborn, however much Augustine might have disavowed that philosophy. Over the course of the next fifteen years, Julian carried on a battle with Augustine that would dwarf any of

Augustine's earlier ones, in both length and ferocity. He would be the last, most intractable opponent of Augustine's old age.

Reading the correspondence between Augustine and Julian can be dreary work. In the course of their conflict, Julian called Augustine a Manichaean, a liar, a cruel old man, and a lonely voice in isolation against the broader Church. For his part, Augustine mocked the married and thirty-year-younger Julian for glorying in his marital bed, his Christian liberty to enjoy pleasure, and his claim to love God's goodness (*Against Julian* 3.14.28).

Yet despite all this, the conflict was mostly not personal, but rather the outworking of deep-rooted theological principles. Indeed, years before, Augustine had sent Julian one of his works on the liberal arts, *On Music*, in hopes that it would be helpful to the young man as he came of age and became established in good instruction. Like Augustine, Julian had enjoyed a background of literary cultivation and sophistication. Also like Augustine, he had become bishop at a young age, and had expressed special concern for the poor of his congregation.

But the Pelagian controversy drove them apart. Julian, in denying original sin, also denied there was any Fall of man, and affirmed that man possessed the same freedom to choose good as he did before Adam's sin. Sin existed, to be sure, but it was external and resistible, rather than the internal "root" asserted by Augustine's doctrine, which Julian thought devalued creation. How, he argued, can the doctrine of original sin be reconciled with a God who is entirely good, and who has created the wonders of the earth, the glories of humanity, and even the blessing of marital sexuality?

Julian's attacks on Augustine were calculated to exploit any misgivings Augustine's readers might have held toward teachings of his that went against accepted opinion. And there were many. Then, as now, it was common to think of infants as innocent—as *not* stained with sin until they acquire it from watching others. Yet Augustine maintained they too were corrupted by sin. Then, as now, men might readily ascribe the *glories* of creation to God, but regard the *miseries* we experience as outside of His plan. Yet

Augustine taught that both good and ill come from the hand of God.

But most of all, Augustine's thoughts on sexual desire became easy targets for Julian. Indeed, the accusation most likely to convince a casual reader was that Augustine denied the goodness of sexuality. After all, in his Manichaean days Augustine had once thought perhaps Adam and Eve's bodily existence was itself a punishment for their sin. To Julian, Augustine's statements on sexuality showed that he still held to such notions.

But Augustine had, in fact, moved far away from these ideas. He now realized that the body was no evil in itself, and that God had created Adam and Eve, and everything in the garden, as good. And even though the world's misery, sadness, and pain were results of Adam's sin, what was remarkable to him was how much beauty God still deigned to give His children. Indeed, even in its pains, creation pointed to the greater glories of heaven and paradise.

Julian, on the other hand, denied any Fall that affected creation, and therefore thought of toils such as painful childbirth as realities that might have been present in God's original creation. Augustine rejected this and mocked any Pelagian "paradise" that still included toilsome labor, suffering, sadness, lust, and so on. This world, insofar as it reflected God's good design, was indeed good, but how much better it would be in days to come!

Furthermore, as hard as it was for Augustine to admit, this good design did include sexual desire. Yet his view differed from his opponent's. Julian held that sexual desire of the flesh (*concupiscentia*) was not, in fact, sin, but was ordained by God toward sexual union. Augustine disagreed, accepting that the desire could be helpfully turned toward procreation, but arguing that the desire *itself* was still a result of the Fall. This basic tenet was one Augustine held most of his life, and yet, as often happens in arguments, his polemic with Julian forced him to clarify his position. By the end of his life, Augustine granted that it might be possible to have a sinless kind of sexual desire in this life, if that desire came in the context of marriage and procreation—which is different than the fleshly desire for sex itself. He even granted that, before the Fall, it may have been possible to have a sexual desire of the flesh that was not sinful (but if it existed, he says, it was always under the control of one's will).

To our modern ears, as to Julian's, Augustine's view may sound inhibited, even repressive. But to characterize his position this way is to underestimate the weight of sexual sin, both in Augustine's life and in our own. To be sure, Augustine's past influenced his doctrine of sexuality in ways he never fully banished, yet his focus on these things comes not from prudishness, but from a deep personal understanding of the heart of man and of God's holiness. "Know thyself; know God." This was the utterance of one of Augustine's first works after his conversion (*Soliloquies*), and it remained with him throughout his life, no more so than in his disputes with the Pelagians.

In the end, Augustine could appreciate Pelagius's zeal for holiness, but not his lack of awareness of his own heart. He could understand Julian's concern about Manichaean pessimism, but not Julian's refusal to know the evil in the hearts of himself and all men. He, as much as the Pelagians or any man, could appreciate the force of habit that binds us to our sin. But unlike them, he was constrained to see in sin more than just bad choices: it was, in fact, bad desires from the corrupted root of Adam's sin.

Augustine's teaching on this point has stood the test of time, and for good reason. His "doctrine of original sin" rests upon the clear testimony of Scripture: "The heart is deceitful above all things, and desperately wicked: who can know it?" (Jer. 17:9). Julian never would accept Augustine's criticisms, and at his death, long after Augustine's, he still opposed the doctrine of original sin. Augustine's critique of him, in the end, boiled down to one point: Julian had many gifts—not least of which his reason—but he thought he knew his heart, and so he did not know it at all.

14

₴

OLD AGE

IN THE WINTER OF 429, Augustine was asked to attend a dedication of a new church. In the past, he had accepted many such invitations, enjoying the chance to travel. But this time, he refused, citing the difficulties of traveling in winter at his age. In a day when life expectancy hovered in the 40s or early 50s (for those who survived childhood), Augustine was now 75 years old, and age had finally begun to leave its mark.

Augustine had long been fascinated by the glories and pains of the human body, and even when those pains became personal, they were a fruitful topic for consideration, and a reminder that pain was a result of the curse that dogged mankind from birth to death: "Human misery, which courses through this life of ours, is a mark of all men, from the first cries of the newborn to the last gasps of the dying; to only the holy and faithful is happiness promised, but in the next life" (*Against Julian, an Unfinished Book* 1.50).

Along with old age had come a growing realization of the limitations of his time and body. Augustine had been giving sermons (multiple per week) for the past thirty-five years at Hippo, yet as he approached 70, he felt the need to pass off this responsibility. Trouble in nearby parishes had reminded him of the need to make careful arrangements for the organization of the church of Hippo after his death, and so he appointed Heraclius, one of his own clergy at Hippo, as his successor. Though Heraclius would not formally be ordained bishop until Augustine's death, he would from 426 onwards assume responsibility for many of the day-to-day tasks of a bishop. Not only did Augustine inform his congregation of this decision, but he also obtained their consent at a special service. Remarkably, he also ensured that the stenographers of Hippo recorded the proceedings. The transcript that we still possess today is remarkable for the intimacy it shows us between a bishop and his congregation:

> I want to announce to all of you my will, which I believe is of God: I wish for the presbyter Heraclius to be my successor.
>
> The people shouted: "Thanks be to God! Praise be to Christ!" twenty-three times. "Hear us, O Christ: Long live Augustine!" was said sixteen times. "You are our father, you are our bishop!" they said eight times.
>
> When it was calm again, Bishop Augustine said: "There's no need for me to say anything in praise of him; I honor his wisdom, and am mindful of his modesty: it is enough that you know him. ... This, then, is what I wish; this is what I plead from the Lord our God in fervent prayers, even now in the chill of old age; this is what I urge, admonish, beg that you pray along with me: that God would gather and join together in the peace of Christ all of our minds, and establish what he has done among us. May He who sent me him also preserve him; may He keep him from harm, keep him free from reproach, so that he who gives me joy while I live may take my place when I die. As you can see, the stenographers of the church are taking down what we say, taking down what you say; both my words and your shouts and cheers are not falling to the ground. To say it more plainly, we are assembling an ecclesiastical record: for I want this to be established as far as it's in man's ability to do.
>
> The people shouted thirty-six times, "Thanks be to God! Praises be to Christ!" "Hear us, O Christ: Long live Augustine!" they said thirteen times. "You are our father; you are our bishop!" they said eight times. "It is worthy and just" they said twenty

times. "Very deserving, very worthy!" they said five times. "It is worthy and just!" they said six times.

When it was calm again, Bishop Augustine spoke: "Therefore, as I was saying, I want my will and your will confirmed in an ecclesiastical record, as far as it's in man's ability to do; but as far as it's up to the hidden will of the Almighty, let us all, as I said, pray that God may establish what he has worked among us."

The people shouted sixteen times, "We give thanks for your judgment!" "So be it, so be it!" they said twelve times. "You are our father, Heraclius is our bishop!" they said six times. (*Letters* 213.1–3)

The handoff of responsibility to Heraclius meant that Augustine was now free to concentrate on other pressing matters: namely, his writing. A number of works remained unfinished, and that many of these were completed in the last four years of Augustine's life we owe to his resignation from active ministry. Commentaries on Genesis, Romans, and other scriptural works; another work against the Arian heresy; his preaching manual *On Christian Teaching*; even *City of God*, perhaps—all of these were finished at the tail end of Augustine's life, in a flurry of activity.

For there was little time, now—not only for Augustine, but also for the united Roman world he had known. Aside from the military dangers made clear by the sack of Rome, the intellectual and cultural world of the Christian Empire was also changing. Now split into West and East, the Empire was becoming splintered and regional, and the Christian world was reflecting this change. Theology had always had regional emphases in the Christian world, but now this was increasing. In the East, Christian culture tended to be urban and philosophical, while in the West, it tilted increasingly toward rural and practical emphases. Even language was showing the change: knowledge of Greek, the common tongue of the East, as well as of Scripture and the Early Church, was becoming rarer in the West. Indeed, Augustine himself was never more than passable at it, and thereby set a precedent for Latin dominance in succeeding generations of churchmen in the

West: if Latin was good enough for Augustine, it was good enough for everyone else.

For across the West, but especially in Africa, Augustine was becoming not only a model for imitation, but a seal of authority and reliability. In the eyes of most men, the days of viewing Augustine as an erratic Manichaean philosopher were long gone. For the last thirty years he had left his mark on Christian theology, preaching, politics, letter writing, and rhetoric, so much so that many of his fellow churchmen seemed content to rely on answers he had given rather than investigate questions for themselves. Thus, among the most natural "successors" of Augustine we tend to find the *doctrine* of Augustine maintained, but little of the intellectual *originality* and *vigor* Augustine had brought. For good and ill, much of Africa (and eventually, the Church at large) was content that if Augustine said it, or did it, or thought about it, or wrote on it, no one else needed to.

Yet critics were still not hard to find. There was Julian, and the Pelagians. Officially, Augustine's position had triumphed, yet questions lingered. Even among Augustine's friends, his intense championing of original sin and the sovereignty of God had brought discomfort, particularly among the monasteries.

Two groups of these concerned friends appear late in Augustine's life. In the monastery of Hadrumentum, Africa, several monks were concerned that Augustine's emphasis on the bondage of sin invalidated any conception of the will's freedom, and destroyed the logical basis for correction or rebuke. Augustine's theology seemed to them a threat to an ecclesiastical order that depended on hierarchy and discipline.

Augustine's emphasis on predestination also raised eyebrows. In the last years of his life, he received questions and objections from a monastery now in southern France. These monks did not question that grace was a free gift from God, but they thought it unnecessary for man's initial belief to be considered part of that grace. God's grace was crucial, of course, but it could be given *in response to* man's decision to believe, as weak as that belief might be.

Augustine's response to these churchmen is measured, yet

intense. Though not rejecting the concept of original sin per se, they nonetheless were unwilling to accept the implications that Augustine now saw everywhere in Scripture. He was not the same man that he was at his conversion in 386. Time, Providence, the reading of Scripture, and debates with men like Julian had convinced him of the utter inability of man, and the utter gloriousness of God's undeserved grace toward man. Anything else was simply not consistent with Scripture.

Much as we might admit the importance of these theological battles, it is nonetheless easy to dismiss Augustine's intensity in these last works as born of stubbornness, fatigue, obsession, or other marks of old age. Many a scholar has found unpalatable the sometimes grim nature of Augustine's writings in these last years.[1] But if the anti-Pelagian works of his old age are sometimes hard pills to swallow, Augustine's overall outlook remains energetic and positive. In his correspondence, Augustine can still be found writing to people in far-distant locales, engaging in both theological and personal issues. His sermons still show the vitality of a man who enjoyed face-to-face contact with his congregation. And the final chapters of works such as *City of God* show the old, characteristic sensitivity to the minutest facets of daily life.

Still, along with such glories, old age inevitably brought Augustine face to face with disappointments. Some were theological and political. Despite the outward Christianity that had graced the Empire for a century now, many elements of it remained resolutely pagan. For one, slavery and brutal treatment of prisoners continued into the early fifth century. Augustine and his longtime friend Alypius worked to oppose this slave trade practiced even by Christians, and to mitigate its sorrows. Late in his career, we can even see Augustine taking time to interview a young girl who had been abducted from her home by slave traders. No quiet retirement for this bishop—Augustine knew firsthand the evils

---

1. Indeed, even Peter Brown has admitted to this; in his revised biography, he notes that, as a young man writing the first edition of the biography, he tended to see a certain shriveling of intellectual horizons or natural affection in the old Augustine. See "New Evidence" in Brown, *Augustine of Hippo*, 441–481.

remaining in a "Christian" empire, and was determined to fight them.

Other disappointments were personal. There was the problem of corrupt military officials so entrenched in political schemes that they neglected their obligation to protect Africa (more on this in the next chapter). Try as he might, Augustine had only limited success convincing them to honor their duty. There was also the burden of unfinished works, many remaining so even at his death (among them, his abandoned treatise on the liberal arts, and his response to Julian). And, of course, there was the lingering sadness of having lost most of his close friends and family in his youth.

And then there were those friends whom Augustine had long urged to embrace Christianity, yet had not. After Augustine's ordination to the ministry, most of the figures of his early life that we read about in *Confessions* never appear again. One exception, though, is Romanianus, Augustine's patron, who had first led him into Manichaeism, but then vanishes from the record—almost.

Sometime in the fifth century (the date is uncertain), Romanianus reappears in a letter Augustine wrote to him. The tone is friendly, somewhat nostalgic, even, yet we learn by its end that Romanianus, despite years of prodding, refuses still to accept the Christianity of his young protégé. The intimacy and disappointment on Augustine's part is palpable:

> If you're going to spurn in your heart the words of a bishop, your friend, whoever he may be, think of the body of your Lord in your body: finally, to what end are you going to sin by putting off [your conversion] from day to day, when you do not know your last day? (*Letters* 259.3)

Such brushes with the past in the aged Augustine are rare, yet do emerge in his late writings. They do so most often in conversation with his few remaining old friends: Alypius, Paulinus of Nola, even Jerome (up until his death in 420). Of Monica, Augustine's dear mother, we hear little, yet even she shows up in a late work.[2]

---

2. *On the Care of the Dead* 16.

And then there is Adeodatus, the son of Augustine's sinful youth, about whom he is so silent all his life. For forty years Augustine says nothing of him, yet, unexpectedly, in his final year of life we glimpse a few passing hints of the father's love, both times through the words of Cicero.

The first allusion pops up in a letter Augustine wrote the last year or so of his life. Augustine's immediate addressee is Firmus, his "publisher" for *City of God*. But Augustine's letter is not professional but personal. He urges Firmus to take the plunge and embrace the Christianity he has admired from afar. He answers Firmus's question about what Greek and Latin works he should use to teach his son. And, in a remarkable disclosure, Firmus's son becomes a sounding board for Augustine's own memories:

> I desire, I wish, I urge that he [Firmus's son] ... choose to please good men rather than most men, and this not only in his words and speeches, but also in his life and deeds. Thus I especially want to know about the aspects of his moral character that please you, so that you may make me too a partaker of your joy in him. For I have no doubt that you would wish him to be better than you in all things. (*Letters* 2*.13)

This final sentence alludes to a letter of Cicero to his own son.[3] It was likely not a famous line, but it represented so much of what Augustine had learned in his lifetime. Classical learning, and the power of words, *were* helpful, and could be used virtuously—but more important was that virtue be possessed *inwardly* through Christ. To this end Augustine had dedicated his life: "I have no greater joy than to hear that my children walk in truth" (3 John 1:4). As a bishop, Augustine surely identified with the Apostle John in this; indeed, it had been Augustine's work as spiritual father, producing *spiritual* sons, that had given back some of what God had taken away physically so long ago.

Some, but not all, for sure. And indeed, it is a mix of pride,

---

3. The original letter has not survived. This is another case where Augustine (apparently without knowing) preserves a fragment from an ancient author, reusing it in a new context.

sadness, and comfort that we see in some of the last paragraphs Augustine ever wrote. A moment ago we saw Augustine as proud father emerge in his letter to Firmus; now, deep in the midst of a furious theological battle with Julian, Augustine is suddenly brought again to these words of Cicero, the mouthpiece for his heart—and for just a moment, we hear perhaps a memory of Augustine's own son and the pride he had in him:

> Did not Cicero give voice to the heart of all fathers when he wrote to his son and said, "Of all men, you are the only one whom I would wish to surpass me in all things." (*Against Julian, an Unfinished Book* 6.22)

The opportunity for a son's successes had been cut tragically short, but Augustine would work to see that his spiritual posterity would have every tool to surpass what he had given them.

Indeed, Augustine would spend most of these final days with a view toward the future. This leads to what is Augustine's final, and in some ways most remarkable, completed work. Entitled *Reconsiderations*, it is, in effect, a complement to *Confessions*. Whereas *Confessions* recounted Augustine's life, *Reconsiderations* focuses on his literary history, with a view to which works, and which aspects of those works, would be most helpful to a future readership. Augustine goes through his entire literary oeuvre piece by piece, giving the date of composition, the subject, and a few comments about each work. Ever the quibbling nitpicker, Augustine is in full obsessive mode in *Reconsiderations,* recalling how he used a slightly incorrect word here, or referenced an obscure incorrect scientific fact there. We also see his extreme sensitivity to the slightest sin: he notes that, in the work *Against the Skeptics*, he used expressions such as "perchance" or "as fortune would have it," whereas now he regrets that such usage did not acknowledge God's providence. We learn, too, how in certain areas, Augustine's views had shifted: the liberal arts, for instance, he once believed could help men "bring out things buried by forgetfulness, and in a way dig them up," but he now believes that the best answers to deep questions come not from education, but to those given the "light of eternal reason" (*Reconsiderations* 1.4.4).[4]

Reconsiderations is thus the work of a man who has changed, and who wishes to use the progress he has made to help others follow his course in loving God. The Augustine of *Reconsiderations* is far removed from the one in the early pages of *Confessions*. That Augustine conceived of Genesis as allegorical—now, Augustine accepts the literal creation of Adam and Eve. That Augustine thought of physicality as a result of the Fall—this Augustine now sees physicality as a good gift of God that has been corrupted. That Augustine saw mostly the sorrows of the created order—the mature Augustine can alongside those sorrows see the glories of creation, which even after the Fall endure as undeserved blessings. And whereas the old Augustine approached Scripture with a need to conform it to his reason, the mature Augustine now accepted the authority of Scripture and of the Church over that of the rational mind. Old age had brought Augustine to less faith in humanity, but to more faith in God, and to a realization that the sins and sorrows of his own life were part of the fabric of a life that was being renewed—and that this life, recounted, criticized, and preserved, could be of use to the world in the uncertain days to come.

---

4. He notes his own oversights, too: in discussing Jesus' ministry, Augustine had earlier argued that Jesus did "nothing by force but all things by persuasion and warning," because it had not occurred to him that Jesus had cleansed the Temple with a whip (*Reconsiderations* 1.13.6).

15

⚘

Death and the End of Roman Hippo

*A*FTER 410, Augustine was under no illusions about the fragility of the Roman world, particularly his home of Africa. Though Africa had long been spared the invasions that had plagued other regions, its security rested on a precariously balanced economic and military arrangement. As the 420s marched on, that arrangement began to break down. For the last decade of his life, military turmoil was the order of the day, and this shed light on how thin was the wall between Roman citizen and barbarian: "For not only on the frontier, but in all the provinces peace is brought about by the oaths of the barbarians" (*Letters* 47.2).

The Roman armies that enforced such oaths were commanded by men whose allegiances could be questioned, and whose moneybags were never full enough. As a result, Augustine increasingly found it necessary to intervene in political and military affairs. In one instance, an official named Count Boniface was wavering on whether to pursue his duties in defense of Africa or his desire to enter Christian ministry. In no uncertain terms, Augustine told him they needed good generals more than monks, and Boniface yielded.

The political situation weighed on Augustine's mind, and brought any number of questions, theories, and dilemmas. Sixteen years earlier,[1] Augustine had wondered how a Christian

---

1. In a meditation on Livy's *History of Rome* (*City of God* 3.20).

people would react to a siege. Would they react with despair, or hope in the promise of eternal life? Augustine thought the latter.

He got to find out for himself in the last year of his life. In the summer of 429, Vandal tribes of Swedish origin crossed the Straits of Gibraltar into Africa. As Roman defenses collapsed, the invasion spread across Roman Africa. It was an invasion of a kind not seen for hundreds of years. Writers of the time said that, compared to these wolf-like Vandals, the earlier Visigothic invaders of Rome had been like sheep.

The Vandal leader, Geiseric, devastated the land:

> And through all the regions of Mauritania and even passing over to our other provinces and locales, raging with every savage ferocity and cruelty, they plundered everything they could by their spoiling, slaughter, tortures of all sorts, infernos, and other uncountable and unspeakable evils: sparing men nor women, old nor young, neither even the presbyters or ministers of God nor the very church adornments or supplies or even the buildings. (*Life* 28)

Cities were destroyed, churches burned, women raped, citizens killed or sold into slavery. What defenses there were seem to have been concentrated on three major cities: Carthage, Cirta, and Augustine's Hippo—and so refugees flocked there from all directions. Others, however, could not flee—so what *should* they do? True to form, this very question was asked of Augustine in the midst of the crisis: What should a faithful bishop do in the face of invasion? Should he stay and face the violence, or was this a time to heed Christ's command to flee approaching judgment? What good was there to remain simply to watch the churches burned, men killed, and women violated?

Augustine's reply was sympathetic but firm. There *were* conditions under which a bishop might consider fleeing, but only when doing so would not deprive his flock of the ministries they needed. Bishops who left their flock without pastoral care and the administration of the sacraments were abandoning their posts and their vows, and proving to be the hirelings the Lord warned against:

> But now as for those who ... are overcome by fear, why do they not rather battle bravely against their fear, with the Lord's mercy and aid, lest incomparably more severe evils, which are much more worthy of fear, come upon them? ... Let us fear more that their inner mind be corrupted and the chastity of their faith perish than that women be violently raped in the flesh.... Let us fear more that the members of Christ's body be slain, deprived of spiritual nourishment, than that the members of our body be seized by an enemy assault and tortured. Not that we ought not avoid these things when we can, but rather that they must be borne when we cannot avoid them without being unfaithful, unless perhaps someone would contend that a minister is not unfaithful who takes away a ministry essential for faithfulness at the moment when it is all the more necessary. (*Letters* 228.7)

Twenty years earlier, calamity had befallen Rome, and no one could agree what it signified. Was it a sign of Christianity's inability to protect Rome? Was it, as Augustine argued, one more in a chain of disasters in the City of Man? Was it a judgment of God upon His people?

Now, the people of Hippo asked the same questions:

> Because of this we often conversed amongst ourselves, and pondered the fearful judgments of God laid before our eyes, saying, *"Righteous are you, O Lord, and your judgment is right."* And with shared grief, in anguish and tears we prayed the Father of mercies and Lord of all consolation that He might see fit to bear us up in this trial. (*Life* 28)

In the winter of 429, the Vandal armies surrounded the city of Hippo. Cut off from the sea, Hippo, with all of its inhabitants and refugees, began to starve and thirst. Now a man of 76, Augustine could do little to help. Three months into the siege, in the summer of 430, sickness took Augustine. He seems to have known he would not recover from it, and that the days ahead were griefs to be allayed only by heaven:

And one day, it happened that, while we were seated with him at the table, and talking together, he said to us, "You should know that, in this time of our distress, I have asked God this: either that He would see fit to free this city, surrounded by its foes—or, if something else seems good to Him, to make His servants strong for deferring to His will—or that at least He might take me out of this world unto Himself." (*Life* 29)

Unlike many Christians of our time (and to some extent his), Augustine treated death neither lightly nor with dread. Instead, what most characterized his attitude in these final days of war was a concern for not just the physical safety but also the spiritual perseverance of men's souls, not least his own. To see such violence in his latter days was painful, but not the worst pain:

> But pondering these things . . . , and discerning in them the perils and deaths of souls especially (since, as it is written, *He who acquires knowledge, acquires grief*, and *An understanding heart is a worm in the bones*), even more than usual, tears were his bread day and night, and he spent and endured what were nearly the last days of his life, which were the most bitter and most sorrowful by far of his old age. (*Life* 28)

This "death of souls" was what drove Augustine now. This was the reason for his intense refusal to allow bishops to flee for their own safety. And this was the reason his last days focused on the need for perseverance in faith. His forty years in the ministry had shown him how many men would start with great faith, yet fall away before the end. Sin was ever present. Even the godliest Christian could not endure without the constant nourishment of grace.

Put simply, there was no assumption on Augustine's part that faith at the approach of death is either inevitable or easy—to die well required work that could not be done by others:

> Now this holy man . . . throughout our conversations had been accustomed to telling us that, after baptism had been received,

even the finest Christians and presbyters ought not leave this life without suitable and fitting repentance. And this practice he himself did in the last sickness in which he died: for indeed he had ordered that the shortest of the penitential Psalms of David be written out for him, and lying in bed in the days of his sickness, he would gaze at and read those sheets placed on the wall, weeping abundantly and without ceasing. (*Life* 31)

On August 26, 430, Augustine of Hippo died at the age of 76. He was buried in Hippo (his grave is unknown to this day), but left no will, for he had few possessions of his own. Among his last instructions were that the library and books of the church of Hippo be preserved for the benefit of future generations. He had toiled forty years among them, and they would be, he hoped, helpful to Christians in an uncertain future.

The siege of Hippo dragged on after Augustine's death. Count Boniface, whom Augustine had urged to fulfill his duty of protection, made a last stab at driving away the invaders, but it was too little, too late. In late 431, Hippo was taken by the Vandals. The church was burned, and the city's residents evacuated. Yet, by a happy act of Providence, Augustine's library somehow survived (we don't know how). His friend Possidius survived too. He gathered all the works of Augustine he could find, compiled a list of most of them, and transmitted it to future generations along with his *Life of Augustine* biography. For those who could not enjoy the benefit of hearing him preach, they were, Possidius said, the best substitute:

> And indeed from his writings it is plain that this presbyter, accepted by and dear to God, lived rightly and soberly in faith, hope, and love of the Catholic Church, as far as he was granted to see these things by the light of truth—which they recognize who profit by reading his writings on divine matters. But for my part, I think those were able to profit more from him who were able to hear and see him personally as he spoke in the church, and who were familiar especially with his daily manner of life among

men. For he was not only a scribe instructed unto the kingdom of heaven, bringing forth from his treasure new things and old, and one of the merchants who, having found a pearl of great price, sold whatever he had and bought it, but indeed also one of those to whom it is written: *So speak, and so do*; and of whom the Savior says: *He who shall so do and teach men, the same shall be called great in the kingdom of heaven.* (*Life* 31)

16

⚜

Legacy

WITHIN A FEW YEARS OF AUGUSTINE'S DEATH, much of the physical fruit of his labors was gone. His church had been burnt, his people scattered or killed, his clergy dispersed, arrested, or killed. Throughout Africa, the churches he had tried to preserve for the Catholic (as opposed to the Donatist) Church had been destroyed. The Empire was Christian, yet still profane in a number of ways, and in the West, poor leadership, military defeats, and economic hardship accompanied an empire in decline. There would be one more generation of Romans before even the illusion of empire would end in 476 as Germanic tribes deposed the last Western emperor.[1] Pelagianism had officially been vanquished, but Augustine's own writings show that threads of it lived on, difficult to stamp out. In tangible terms, there was little to show for forty years of work.

Yet Augustine himself could never have anticipated what fruit God would bring from his life. He could never have known that his work on the Trinity would echo far beyond his time, becoming the West's definitive source on Trinitarian thought. He could never have known that his attempt to vindicate Christianity in *City of God* would provide a blueprint for medieval society, to be seized upon by Charlemagne and others within four hundred years after his death. He could not have anticipated that his little

1. That being said, "Romanness" did not suddenly end in 476. Many continued to conceive of themselves and their culture as Roman for many years into the future.

booklet *Enchiridion* (*A Handbook on Faith, Hope, and Love*) would help in later years to define what aspects of doctrine were central ("in essentials, unity—in doubtful matters, liberty—in all things, charity"). And he certainly could not have known that his tireless emphasis on the radical corruption of sin and the unconditional sovereignty of God would be the hallmark of his theology for both his lovers and his haters.

Already, by Augustine's death, his writings were circulating throughout Africa and beyond. In the coming centuries, his influence was felt in every genre in which he had written. Monastic writers such as Prosper of Aquitaine perpetuated his theological emphases, though blunting some of their force (e.g., on Pelagianism). Preachers such as the sixth-century Eugippius of Italy used Augustine's sermons as models for their own, even copying wholesale portions directly (our conception of plagiarism is a modern one). Teachers and encyclopedists such as Cassiodorus and Isidore of Seville mined for their own works the sheer bulk and variety of Augustine's interests and commentary, and thereby ensured his works' survival along with their own. And, on the furthest edge of the known world, an Irish monk named Hibernicus found that Augustine's name itself was what was most important. He knew no one had heard of *Hibernicus*, so he needed a pen name; and to grant his works a wide audience, he chose *Augustinus*. This was the name that would gain the widest, most authoritative hearing among the audience Hibernicus anticipated.

Augustine, the African writer, had become Augustine the Authority, and for men of the Middle Ages and beyond, that was enough:

> He lies who says he has read you completely.
> Or what reader can possess all your works?
> For in a thousand volumes you shine, O Augustine;
> Your books bear witness of what I say of you.
> However satisfying it is to have books by many authors,
> If Augustine is at hand, he will be enough for you.[2]

---

2. Isidore of Seville, *On the Nature of Things*, in *Patrologia Latina* 83:1109.

To be sure, this kind of reflexive reliance on Augustine's authority had its own downfalls. For starters, it meant that even though Augustine's constant refrain is that readers *not* follow him into error, later generations at times did just that. This happened in matters of Scripture: his failure to follow Jerome's lead in distinguishing the Old Testament apocryphal books from canonical ones meant that Jerome's careful distinction was often lost on future ages.[3] It also took place in matters of anthropology: his incautious treatment on the question of relics[4] contributed to much future superstition and relic cults.

Then, too, there were the areas where Augustine's own skill had unforeseen and unintended results. There was his appeal to the bishop of Rome, for instance, in stamping out heresy; by itself, it was a master move, but it set a precedent for Rome's preeminence in both dignity (which Augustine might have accepted) and power (which he likely would not have) that cast a long shadow over the next thousand years. The idea of an infallible "pope," unthinkable to churchmen of Augustine's day, gained considerable steam because of Augustine's use of Rome's authority.

Even Augustine's own spiritual growth could have unintended consequences. As we have noted, one way of understanding Augustine's growth is to see his growing acceptance of physical, *created* realities. As his mind moved from philosophy to Scripture, so it could see that the practical, the earthy, even the mundane, could all be acceptable in the sight of God. So far, so good. But for later generations, it was possible to err in the other direction. The physical could also overshadow the spiritual, so that godliness consisted of externalism, of keeping the outside clean but ignoring spiritual realities, of mechanizing the Christian life. And indeed, the Church of the Middle Ages is full of this dynamic, of

---

3. The Jews held the apocryphal books on a lower level than their canonical books. In the 400s, when Jerome produced his new translation/revision of the Latin Bible (the so-called *Vulgate*), he included the apocryphal books in it, but noted he did not accord them canonical status. Augustine comments little on this, but quotes freely from the apocryphal books, evidently according them equal authority.

4. See *On the Care of Dead*, which, though mostly very helpful, is too uncritical on the question of miraculous properties of dead saints.

an ever-expanding sacramental system where countless physical acts are assumed to accomplish spiritual realities invariably and mechanistically.

Such a development Augustine would have hated. His goal was to champion the everyday Christian, not diminish the role of faith and affection in him. No doubt had he seen where this emphasis would take the Church, he would have thought it prudent to adjust course. But of course hindsight belongs to posterity.

And indeed, if Augustine was in some ways the architect of the Middle Ages, he also was the inspiration for the Reformation. Both Martin Luther and John Calvin championed Augustine against medieval philosophers and theologians, valuing his submission to Scripture, emphasis on faith, and commitment to the absolute sovereignty of God. Luther's *Bondage of the Will* is unthinkable without Augustine's influence, and Calvin's *Institutes* quotes him more than any other extrabiblical source.

Even the modern world owes much to Augustine. History, as a discipline, is hardly comprehensible apart from *City of God*. In philosophy, Augustine is the principle channel through which Plato's ideas came into the Western world, just as Aquinas (who consciously drew from Augustine) was for Aristotle years later. Military theorists have seen Augustine as the architect of just war theory, a topic increasingly relevant in a world of nuclear arms, women combatants, and drone warfare. Linguistics have found fertile ground for conceptions such as semiotics in Augustine's notions of the nature of language. Psychologists have long been attracted to the complex inner world of Augustine, particularly his subtle insights into childhood expressions and emotions. And Augustine's musings and theories on time in the last chapters of *Confessions* have new life in the post-Einsteinian world of relativity, as physicists have asked the same question that Augustine struggled to answer: What is time?

Note the irony: Augustine spent his first thirty years in an intense, painful search for success in every area the world valued. In schooling. In learning. In teaching rhetoric. In serving at the highest levels of government. And of course, even in genuine love, and in the son that came from it. And he *achieved* success in each of them. Yet each of these things he eventually had to give up. When Augustine let go of these things at his conversion (and later ordination), it was not a half-hearted, temporary discarding. There was no hope that worldly success of that kind would return to him. And return it did not.

Yet in a larger sense, it did. Giving up his life to the demands of God meant death to all things he had known, yet also life and rest such as he had *never* known. Of all men, Augustine had learned that the things we fear to lose are granted when we lose them to God. By giving up each of these things, he regained them for eternity. "Cast your bread upon the waters: for you will find it after many days" (Eccl. 11:1)—Augustine surely affirmed the truth of this verse, but could not see its outworking in his time. Today, fifteen hundred years later, it is clear.

And this brings us to the letter that began this book, written from Augustine to Count Darius amid the Vandals' invasion of North Africa in 429. It is odd that Augustine's last surviving letter is not to a distant, influential bishop, not to the monasteries whose scribes held the future to Augustine's legacy, not even to a lifelong friend like Alypius. Rather, it is to an imperial official, one whose actions weighed heavily on Hippo's fate, yet one to whom Augustine hardly mentions their military crisis.

Instead, we read gentle reminiscences of a shared classical training, one Augustine had partly put away years ago as the relics of an old, dying world. *That* Augustine had felt the discord between Cicero and Christ, between his classical upbringing and newfound faith. But *this* Augustine had imbibed Scripture for some forty years now, and in the process had finally gained a mature perspective on how a Christian could regard the past—both the past of classical antiquity, and the past of his own life. As he had noted in *On Christian Teaching,* his manual for preachers, a Christian grounded in the faith could glean profitably from the "spoil of the Egyptians" found in pagan works. For a man who now held total allegiance to Scripture, quoting a pagan author like Themistocles was no longer a hindrance to a living, vital faith in Christ.

Nor was his own past any longer a stumbling block. The young Augustine had been a wash of ambition and insecurities, of inclinations toward righteousness without the power to achieve it, and of constant battles with the flesh. But as he moved toward death, and as his city was being besieged, Augustine was a different man. The spiritual perils of his prior life lay in the past. They were not eradicated, since (he would stress) no sin ever is in this life—but nonetheless they lay on the other side of forty years of sanctification. Now, Augustine had some sense that the wanderings of his earlier life were not an embarrassing prelude to his life, but a useful part of it.

Looking back on his young life, Augustine could see the waste of years, but he also saw God's hand in them. If the young Augustine had shown feet of clay, the mature Augustine knew it was the Potter's right to mold that clay for His will, and His pleasure, and on His timetable. For thirty years, he had grown to learn how his own failures could be a teaching tool for others, and as an old man of 76, that process had reached its conclusion. Augustine had made errors, but also learned from his errors:

> Therefore let whoever reads these works not imitate me when I err, but rather when I make progress toward the better. For perhaps whoever reads my little works in the order in which I wrote them will discover how I made progress by writing. (*Reconsiderations*, prologue, sec. 3)

Understanding this brings clarity to this last letter of Augustine. Giving his autobiography to this military official may seem strange, yet it is, in effect, Augustine's offering of himself, of all his sins, and all his glories, and all his peculiarities, for the benefit of this man he scarcely knew. *Confessions* symbolizes how God had restored the things that Augustine had tried so hard not to lose. And it represents Augustine's final understanding of the value of a soul. Darius was valuable in his efforts to save Africa from destruction, yet this paled in comparison to the value of his eternal soul. From Romanianus to Julian, Monica to Marcellinus, and Boniface to

Darius, Augustine strives in his conversations and dialogues to bring the reality of eternity into daily life. When all is said and done, confession of sin and praise to God is the best summary Augustine can offer of his life. No higher honor, no more abiding legacy, could he give than this epitaph; and so it is with these words that we close this biography:

> Accept then, my son, ... accept, I say, the books of my *Confessions* that you wished for: there examine me, lest you praise me beyond what I am; there believe not others about me but me myself; there consider, and see what I have been in myself, through myself; and if anything in me pleases you, praise along with me there not me, but Him whom I have wanted to be praised on my account. *For He Himself made us, and not we ourselves*; indeed, we had destroyed ourselves, but he who made us, made us anew. (*Letters* 231.6)

APPENDIX A

WHERE TO GO FROM HERE?

TO LEARN MORE ABOUT AUGUSTINE, there is no substitute for digging in and reading the man himself. The traditional recommendation is to start with *Confessions*, and this is sound advice. (I've included a classic excerpt for you as Appendix B below.) Nothing immerses you in the history, thought, and inner life of Augustine as this work does. The final chapters are (spoiler alert!) tough sledding (Augustine contemplates the meaning of time), but worthwhile nonetheless.

From there, the choices diverge, but one cannot go wrong by reading a larger biography of the bishop of Hippo. By necessity, this book has presented only the barest outline of Augustine's life, and filling in this outline with a comprehensive biography will pay great dividends in further study of Augustine.

You might start with the shortest, and first, biography, written by Augustine's friend and fellow bishop Possidius. It was he who was responsible for collecting Augustine's works after his death, and passing to posterity his memories of all the things Augustine chose not to include in *Confessions* (especially his work as a bishop). An excellent translation is available in the public domain, and readily online.

But to really get a sense of Augustine and his world, the classic choice is Peter Brown's magisterial biography. First completed in the early 1960s, it revolutionized the world of anyone who knew, wrote on, or studied Augustine, and it has never been bettered since. Brown revised it in 2000, and to great benefit for the student. Reading Brown speak of where he has changed his mind, where he was wrong, where he misjudged Augustine, and where new evidence has taken him, is a fascinating, humbling, and edifying experience. If you can read only one work *about* Augustine, this is the one.

What if you just want to know what Augustine thought on a given topic? As I mentioned earlier, this has a long and illustrious tradition among churchmen, encyclopedists, and generally anyone who wanted an authoritative opinion on a subject. Thankfully, unlike medieval scribes, students looking for Augustine's opinion need not search the world to wade through all his works! They need only consult *Augustine Through the Ages: An Encyclopedia*. Here, alphabetized by topic, are short summaries of Augustine's thought and life, as well as how those affected later writers and movements. Want to know about Augustine's views on abortion? It's here (hint: he utterly opposed it). On just war? It's here. On how Aquinas, Luther, and Calvin approached him? Also here. This really does have the potential to be the first stop in studying Augustine on a subject.

Finally, I include here a brief synopsis of all the genres in which Augustine wrote. Since there are so many works within each genre, for each one I've also given a recommended work to start with. Some of these can be found readily online for free, in good (though old) translations. For those wanting a more modern translation, New City Press and the Augustinian Heritage Institute are working on the first translation and publication of all of Augustine's works into English. Begun in 1990, 43 of 49 volumes have now been completed. This is the place to go for reading an uncommon (and often unavailable online) work of Augustine.

Philosophical Treatises

In the brief period after his conversion but before his baptism, Augustine wrote several short philosophical works. Some of these were intended to convince skeptics of the truth of Christianity (*Against the Skeptics, On the Immortality of the Soul*); others were on education (*On the Teacher*) or finding happiness in life (*On the Happy Life*). In *Soliloquies* (Augustine probably coined this word), Augustine tries to find truth by dialoguing with himself; and in *On Music* he outlines a planned liberal arts curriculum (one he never finished). All of these works reveal Augustine as a Christian, but one more acquainted with philosophy than Scripture.

START WITH: *Soliloquies*
RECOMMENDED TRANSLATION: Starbuck (older, online); Paffenroth (New City Press)

Biographical Works

Most famous here is *Confessions*, written right after Augustine's ordination as bishop. It is a work unlike any other—an autobiography that's also an inner meditation on praising God by recounting one's life and sins. Modeled heavily after the Psalms in its style and structure, it is Augustine at his most personal.

Equally unique, but far more straightforward, is Augustine's *Reconsiderations*. Written a few years before his death, here he reviews and dates most of his works. He also steps into the role of self-critic, pointing out in excruciating detail not only errors that he now regrets, but also alleged errors that actually are not. The book is remarkable for showing Augustine's changes on various issues, and consistency on others.

START WITH: *Confessions*
RECOMMENDED TRANSLATION: Unlike with most of Augustine's works, the reader is spoiled for choice here. There are at least ten translations readily available, many of which have particular virtues. For accuracy, beauty, and readability, however, best on balance is the one by F. J. Sheed, available fairly inexpensively. If cost is the highest concern, the translation by J. G. Pilkington is in the public domain and available free online. Finally, if ease of reading and modern language is of highest concern, Henry Chadwick's translation is respected, modern, and inexpensive.

APPENDIX A

Anti-heretical Writings

Works in this category stem from all parts of Augustine's long career, from early anti-Manichaean writings, to works against the Donatists (*On Baptism*), Pelagians (*On Nature and Grace*), Semi-Pelagians (*On the Predestination of the Saints*), and Arians. There are also a variety of works written throughout his life defending the Christian faith against attack on broad (*City of God*) or narrow (*On the Advantage of Believing*) fronts.
START WITH: *City of God* (but be prepared: it's long!)
RECOMMENDED TRANSLATIONS: Marcus Dods (online); William Babcock (New City Press)

Scriptural Treatises and Commentaries

Augustine wrote extended works on large sections of Scripture. He treated Genesis no fewer than five times (most extensively in his work *On the Literal Interpretation of Genesis*), and wrote extensively on the gospel and first epistle of the Apostle John. His masterpiece in this category, however, is indisputably the *Expositions on the Psalms*, which is overwhelming in length, subtlety, and scope. It is among the most important works ever written on the Psalms.
START WITH: *Expositions on the Psalms* (begin by looking at a specific Psalm)
RECOMMENDED TRANSLATIONS: J. E. Tweed (online); Maria Boulding (New City Press)

Theological and Moral Works

Here belong some of the most famous and influential works Augustine composed. Most monumental is his *On the Trinity*, composed over a fifteen-year period and as brilliant and intricate as any work he ever wrote. In it, Augustine elaborates and restates the orthodox, Nicene, and scriptural position on the Trinity, but also breaks new ground by attempting to find analogies of the Trinity in mankind's present existence. His attempt to locate an imprint of the Trinity in the soul of man is one of the headiest and most dizzying undertakings he ever pursued.

Equally influential among his theological works is his *On Christian Teaching*. Far less abstract, and much more practically focused than *On the Trinity*, the work is a handbook of how Christians should view rhetoric, and particularly how pastors should use it in their preaching. As such, the work was greatly influential on subsequent generations of pastors in the Middle Ages and beyond.
START WITH: *On Christian Teaching*
RECOMMENDED TRANSLATIONS: James Shaw (online); Edmund Hill (New City Press)

Christian Life / Moral Works

Here are a variety of other works, including treatises on marriage (*On the Good of Marriage*), burial (*On the Care of the Dead*), monasticism (*On Holy Virginity*), and the very practical work *On Lying*. Last but not least, Augustine's *Enchiridion* (*A Handbook on Faith, Hope, and Love*) compresses all of the Christian faith into a short handbook of great value for Christians both new and old.
START WITH: *Enchiridion* (*A Handbook on Faith, Hope, and Love*)
RECOMMENDED TRANSLATIONS: J. F. Shaw (online); Bruce Harbert (New City Press)

Letters

Over three hundred of these have survived, and they give us an intimate perspective of Augustine's life and career from his conversion to his death in 430. It is no exaggeration to say that every part of Augustine is represented by his *Letters*, and as they continue to be unearthed (the most recent discovery was in the late 1970s), they shed more and more light on the fine points of Augustine's life.
START WITH: Letter 130 to Proba (Augustine explains the Lord's Prayer to her)
RECOMMENDED TRANSLATIONS: J. G. Cunningham (online, but not all letters available); Roland Teske (New City Press)

APPENDIX A

Sermons

These vary in length depending on the length of Augustine's preaching on any particular Sunday, and their themes vary from expositional (sequential treatment of scriptural texts) to topical. They show Augustine at his most colloquial and improvisational.
START WITH: Sermon 81, in which Augustine helps his congregation process through their anxiety about the sack of Rome in 410
RECOMMENDED TRANSLATIONS: R. G. MacMullen (online, but only contains about 25% of the sermons); Edmund Hill (New City Press)

APPENDIX B

Augustine and the Pears

From *Confessions* 2.4.9, 2.6.12–2.10.18:

2.4.9. Theft is punished by Your law, O Lord, and by the law written in men's hearts, which iniquity itself cannot blot out. For what thief will put up with a thief? Even a rich thief will not endure him who is driven to it by want. Yet I had a desire to commit robbery, and did so, compelled neither by hunger, nor poverty through a distaste for well-doing, and an abundance of iniquity. For I stole that of which I already had enough, and much better. Nor did I desire to enjoy what I pilfered, but the theft and sin itself. There was a pear-tree close to our vineyard, heavily laden with fruit, which was tempting neither for its color nor its flavor. To shake and rob this some of us worthless young men went, late one night (having, according to our disgraceful habit, prolonged our games in the streets until then), and carried away great loads, not to eat ourselves, but to fling to the very swine, having only eaten some of them; and to do this pleased us all the more because it was not permitted. Behold my heart, O my God; behold my heart, which You had pity upon when in the bottomless pit. Behold, now, let my heart tell You what it was seeking there, that I should be gratuitously evil, having no inducement to evil but the evil itself. It was foul, and I loved it. I loved to perish. I loved my own error—not that for which I erred, but the error itself. Oh foul soul, falling from Your firmament to utter destruction—not seeking anything through the shame but the shame itself!

...

2.6.12. What was it, then, that I, miserable one, so loved in you, O theft of mine, O deed of darkness, in that sixteenth year of my age? Beautiful you were not, since you were theft. But are you anything, that I may argue the case with you? Those pears that we stole were fair to the sight, because they were Your creation, O Fairest of all, Creator of all, O good God—God, the highest good, and my true good. Those pears truly were pleasant to the sight; but it was not for them that my miserable soul lusted, for I had abundance of better, but those I plucked simply that I might steal. For, having plucked them, I threw them away, my sole gratification in them being my own sin, which I was pleased to enjoy. For if any of these pears entered my mouth, the sweetener of it was my sin in eating it. And now, O Lord my God, I ask what it was in that theft of mine that caused me such delight; and behold it has no beauty in it—not such, I mean, as exists in justice and wisdom; nor such as is in the mind, memory, senses, and animal life of man; nor yet such as is the glory and beauty of the stars in their courses; or the earth, or the sea, teeming with incipient life, to replace, as it is born, that which decays; nor, indeed, that false and shadowy beauty which pertains to deceptive vices.

2.6.13. For thus doth pride imitate high estate, whereas You alone are God, high above all. And what does ambition seek but honors and renown, whereas You alone are to be honored above all, and renowned for evermore? The cruelty of the powerful wishes to be feared; but who is to be feared but God only, out of whose power what can be forced away or withdrawn—when, or where, or to where, or by whom? The charms of the indulgent desire to be loved; but nothing is more enticing than Your charity, nor is anything loved more healthfully than Your truth, bright and beautiful above all. Curiosity affects a desire for knowledge, whereas it is You who supremely know all things. Ignorance, too, and foolishness themselves are concealed under the names of guilelessness and harmlessness, because nothing can be found more guileless than You; and what is more harmless, since it is a sinner's own works by which he is harmed? And sloth seems to long for rest; but what sure rest is there besides the Lord? Luxury craves to be called plenty and abundance; but You are the fullness and unfailing plenteousness of unfading joys. Prodigality presents a shadow of liberality; but You are the most lavish giver of all good. Covetousness desires to possess much; and You are the Possessor of all things. Envy contends for excellence; but what is so excellent as You? Anger seeks revenge; who avenges more justly than You? Fear shudders at unexpected and sudden chances which threaten things that are loved, and is wary for their security; but what can happen that is unexpected or sudden to You? or who can deprive You of what You love? or where is there unshaken security save with You? Grief languishes for things lost in which desire had delighted itself, even because it would have nothing taken from it, as nothing can be from You.

2.6.14. Thus the soul commits fornication when she turns away from You, and seeks outside of You what she cannot find pure and untainted until she returns to You. Thus all pervertedly imitate You who separate themselves far from You and raise themselves up against You. But even by thus imitating You they acknowledge You to be the Creator of all nature, and so that there is no place whither they can altogether retire from You. What, then, was it that I loved in that theft? And wherein did I, even corruptedly and pervertedly, imitate my Lord? Did I wish, if only by artifice, to act contrary to Your law, because by power I could not, so that, being a captive, I might imitate an imperfect liberty by doing with impunity things I was not allowed to do, by a shadowy resemblance to Your omnipotence? Behold this servant of Yours, fleeing from his Lord, and following a shadow! O rottenness! O monstrosity of life and profundity of death! Could I be pleased by that which was unlawful only because it was unlawful?

2.7.15. "What shall I render unto the Lord," that while my memory recalls these things my soul is not appalled at them? I will love You, O Lord, and thank You, and confess unto Your name, because You have put away from me these so wicked and nefarious acts of mine. To Your grace I attribute it, and to Your mercy, that You have melted away my sin as it were ice. To Your grace also I attribute whatever evil I have not committed; for what might I not have committed, loving as I did the sin for the sin's sake? And I confess that all has been pardoned me, both that which I committed by my own perverseness, and that which, by Your guidance, I committed not. Where is he who, reflecting upon his own infirmity, dares to ascribe his chastity and innocence to his own strength, so that he should love You the less, as if he had been in less need of Your mercy, whereby You forgive the transgressions of those that turn to You? For whoever, called by You, obeyed Your voice, and shunned those things which he reads me recalling and confessing of myself, let him not despise me, who, being sick, was healed by that same Physician by whose aid it was that he was not sick, or rather was less sick. And for this let him love You as much, yea, all the more, since the One who has restored me from so great a feebleness of sin is the One who has preserved him from a like feebleness.

2.8.16. "What fruit had I then," wretched one, in those things which, when I remember them, cause me shame—above all in that theft, which I loved only for the theft's sake? And as the theft itself was nothing, all the more wretched was I who loved it. Yet by myself alone I would not have done it—I recall what my heart was—alone I could not have done it. I loved, then, in it the companionship of my accomplices with whom I did it. I did not, therefore, love the theft alone—yea, rather, it was that alone that I loved, for the companionship was nothing. What is the fact? Who is it that can teach me, but He who illumines my heart and searches out its dark corners? What is it that has come into my mind to inquire about, to discuss, and to reflect upon? For had I at that time loved the pears I stole, and wished to enjoy them, I might have done so alone, if I could have been satisfied with the mere commission of the theft by which my pleasure was secured; and not have provoked that itching of my own passions, by the encouragement of accomplices. But as my enjoyment was not in those pears, it was in the crime itself, which the company of my fellow sinners produced.

2.9.17. By what feelings, then, was I animated? For it was in truth too shameful; and woe was me who had it. But still what was it? "Who can understand his errors?" We laughed, because our hearts were tickled at the thought of deceiving those who little imagined what we were doing, and would have vehemently disapproved of it. Yet, again, why did I so rejoice in this, that I did it not alone? Is it that no one readily laughs alone? No one does so readily; but yet sometimes, when men are alone by themselves, nobody being by, a fit of laughter overcomes them when anything very amusing presents itself to their senses or mind. Yet alone I would not have done it—alone I could not at all have done it. Behold, my God, the lively recollection of my soul is laid bare before You—alone I would not have committed that theft, in which what I stole pleased me not, but rather the act of stealing; nor to have done it alone would I have liked so well, neither would I have done it. O Friendship too unfriendly, seducer of the soul, greediness to do mischief out of sport and trifle, craving for others' loss, without desire for my own profit or revenge; but when they say, "Let us go, let us do it," we are ashamed not to be shameless.

2.10.18. Who can unravel that twisted and tangled knottiness? It is foul. I hate to reflect on it. I hate to look on it. But I do long for you, O righteousness and innocence, fair and comely to all virtuous eyes, and of an unsatisfied satisfaction! With you is perfect rest, and life unchanging. He who enters into you enters into the joy of his Lord, and shall have no fear, and shall do excellently in the most Excellent. I sank away from You, O my God, and I wandered too far from You, my stay, in my youth, and became to myself an unfruitful land.

APPENDIX C

TIMELINE OF IMPORTANT EVENTS

Roman and Biblical History

753 BC	Traditional date for the founding of Rome
509	Overthrow of Rome's last king, and beginning of the Roman Republic
44	Julius Caesar assassinated
30	End of the Roman Republic as Octavian becomes the first Roman emperor, later taking the title "Augustus"
c. 4	Birth of Jesus Christ in Bethlehem of Judea
AD 30–33	Crucifixion and resurrection of Jesus
40–50	Traditional date for the arrival of the Evangelist Mark in Alexandria, Egypt; beginning of African Christianity
64–65	Arrest and martyrdom of the Apostles Peter and Paul
70	Destruction of the Temple in Jerusalem
200	The Church Father Tertullian begins his Christian writings in Carthage
250–260	The Decian persecution: widescale persecution and martyrdom of Christians, including Africans such as Origen and Cyprian
303–311	The Great Persecution of Diocletian

TIMELINE OF IMPORTANT EVENTS

Oct 27, 312	Claiming he has seen a sign from Christ in heaven, Constantine wins a decisive battle at Milvian Bridge
Mar 313	Constantine issues the Edict of Milan, granting toleration to Christianity
Sep 18, 323	Constantine defeats Licinius (emperor of the East) to become sole emperor of Rome
337	Upon the death of Constantine, the Empire is split among his children: Constans in the West, and Constantius II in the East; the latter becomes sole emperor in 350

Augustine

Birth and Childhood

AD 354	Augustine (Aurelius Augustinus) born November 13 in Thagaste, Numidia, in North Africa (today Souk Ahras in Algeria)
354–365	Education begins at rhetorical schools in Thagaste
371	Age 17, goes to Carthage to study; spends time at the theater, with unruly friends, and takes up with a woman out of wedlock
372	Son Adeodatus born; father dies, baptized as a Christian on his deathbed; begins to follow the Manichaean sect
373	Under the influence of Cicero's *Hortensius*, begins to search for wisdom through philosophy

Career in Teaching and Rhetoric

374	Returns home to Africa to begin teaching career; opens own school of rhetoric, but finds the antics of the students intolerable
383	Leaves Africa for Rome, hoping for better teaching opportunities; comes into contact with city leader named Symmachus, who chooses Augustine for a prestigious position as professor of rhetoric in Milan, Italy

APPENDIX C

Conversion and New Life

384	Arrives in Milan, where he meets Ambrose, the bishop of the city; Ambrose introduces him to the Neoplatonist philosophers, which cause him to lose confidence in Manichaean teachings; Ambrose helps him overcome "hang-ups" about the Bible using Neoplatonic interpretation, and Augustine decides to become a "learner" in the Church
385	Marriage arranged by Monica, requiring that he end his fourteen-year relationship with the mother of his son; Augustine devastated, but forced to comply; unable to endure a two-year celibacy period, he takes another woman, but is in deep conflict with his growing spiritual understanding
386	Final conversion
387	Death of mother Monica
388	Returns to hometown of Thagaste with friend Alypius and son Adeodatus, disposes of his property, and begins a life of monastic, contemplative study
390	Death of son Alypius

Church Life at Hippo

391	Ordained presbyter at Hippo
393–405	Writes against the Manichaean heresy
394–402	Writes and preaches against the Donatist heresy
396	Becomes sole bishop of Hippo, an office he holds until his death
397	Begins work on *Confessions*, which he works on for the next four years
399	Begins work on his greatest theological work, *On the Trinity*, which occupies the next twenty years of his writing
410	Rome sacked and burned by the Goths, eastern Germanic peoples led by their general Alaric; the resulting looting, violence, terror, and cannibalism shock citizens of the Empire; many lay blame at the feet of Christianity

TIMELINE OF IMPORTANT EVENTS

413	Begins thirteen years of writing his greatest work, *City of God*, prompted by charges that Christianity is to blame for Rome's troubles; it is a vindication of Christianity and interpretation of all of history in Christian terms
418	Leads two hundred bishops in Council of Carthage, which pronounces Pelagianism heretical

Final Years

426	Names Heraclius as his successor and begins to transition away from active ministry
429	Vandal tribes pour into North Africa, burning churches, pillaging cities, and torturing and raping citizens; many refugees flee to Hippo for safety
430	Dies on August 28; Hippo is burned, his church partly destroyed; yet his library is preserved, from which all known manuscripts of Augustine have come

www.ingramcontent.com/pod-product-compliance
Lightning Source LLC
Chambersburg PA
CBHW030155100526
44592CB00009B/289